AF226418

Crafting Green Waves - Radical, efficient, cheap, effective ways to prevent congestion and reduce trip time - 2021 Edition

Overview - Free flow, no bus lanes, conflicts in parallel, choice of priority, quality operation

Preventing congestion permits free flow for all, allows signal linking that reduces delay for the bus, is better than a bus lane, and the alternative of a bus lane seriously congests all other traffic without reason.

Having turn arrows at intersections wastes time for all traffic, creates unsafe driver challenges, and is better **replaced by cross-overs** before the intersection, that move the turns to service roads. .

Free entry to congested roads manages demand by queue delay, yet does not prevent giving all traffic the **choice of jumping the queue** for a toll. Getting most people to jump the queue saves time and keeps the toll as low as possible.

These things serve the travelling public, nobody does them, but job security should be at risk.

Use traffic signals to gate traffic and operate the street in green waves at the speed limit and remove bus lanes. In the counter-peak direction, smooth flow at minor crossings.

Increase intersection capacity by 70% by processing right turn conflicts on the intersections' approaches in parallel with running the cross traffic, so averting intersection turn arrows.

Treat most traffic as a priority by giving them a choice between free entry and a toll. The toll must be set so low as to attract 90%.

Crashes would be halved. Emissions would be halved. Exampled trip times would reduce from 40 minutes to 8 minutes. Pedestrian crossing delays would be halved. Bus priority would be improved.

Conventional intersections are relatively dangerous, risk litigation and should be remodelled at modest cost. **Customers hate congestion**.

Example Route. The most well-known congestion in Melbourne is at the city end of the Eastern Freeway that terminates at Hoddle St and Alexandra Pde. Hoddle St runs south along the eastern side of the city area and Alexandra Pde runs west across the north side. For clarity, only the southbound traffic in the AM peak period will be discussed in this example yet it is also customary to model traffic for both directions in both peak periods and to consider off-peak traffic. The route as mapped from the Eastern Freeway at the Yarra River in Alphington and down the congested Hoddle St - Punt Rd route to the river at Cremorne, **now takes 40 minutes** in the AM peak period and that duration would grow over time **but can be reduced to 8 minutes with no future growth!** Hoddle St from the Eastern Freeway to Victoria Pde has 4 lanes, drawn as the middle arrow, including a peak hour bus lane. 40 buses per hour from the Doncaster area travel the freeway shoulder, down the Hoddle St bus lane, then to the Melbourne CBD along Victoria Pde.

From the north, another 5 buses per hour travel south along all of Hoddle St and Punt Rd, but south of Victoria Pde there are 3 congested lanes with no bus priority.

Existing Failings. The traffic flow volumes and trip speeds for the Hoddle Street - Punt Road route are far below the desirable standards for the existing road width. The existing road **capacity provided is only 44%** of what can be achieved within the existing footprint. The existing trip time is **40 minutes when it could be 8 minutes**.

Mandate NO Congestion & NO Bus Lane. We do not wish to drive in, nor to have the bus in congested traffic. The first step is to constrain flow to below congestion level and to accept that excess demand will readily transfer to the bus. For this, we gate or meter traffic down to practical capacity, reducing flow by only 10%. At practical capacity, we can and would link signals in the peak direction and produce a green wave, that not only gives the bus a free run between intersections, like a bus lane, but linking also reduces bus delay at intersections.

A bus lane reduces the road capacity by 25%, or 33% depending upon the number of lanes available, but with no extra benefits for the bus, so it should be removed. Does capacity matter? If we reduce capacity by 25%, less traffic will depart the queue at the entry gate and nominally the remaining queue will be delayed for 15 minutes (25% of an hour) for every hour of gating the queue. Bus lanes and the congestion that they cause are installed because the alternative of metering is traditionally an unrewarded effort. **Bus lane removal is justified everywhere, gating traffic should be mandatory where there is congestion, and green waves should be a key performance indicator.**

At Victoria St, the practical capacity for a "Two-Phase" intersection should be 5,240 vph (vehicles per hour), but the existing practical capacity is only 2,289 vph (44%). A Two Phase (2Pi) intersection has no turn arrows at the intersection, as detailed later. The traffic signals recorded a congested 3,341 vph. Hoddle St is congested north of

Victoria St, and queues shuffle back through the signals at Langridge St, Gipps St, Johnston St and the Eastern Freeway, a distance of 2km, and spill back on to the Eastern Freeway for a further 2km from 6.30AM to 9.30AM weekdays. A priority lane is provided on the left hand freeway shoulder for free use by buses and selected government cars to jump the queue.

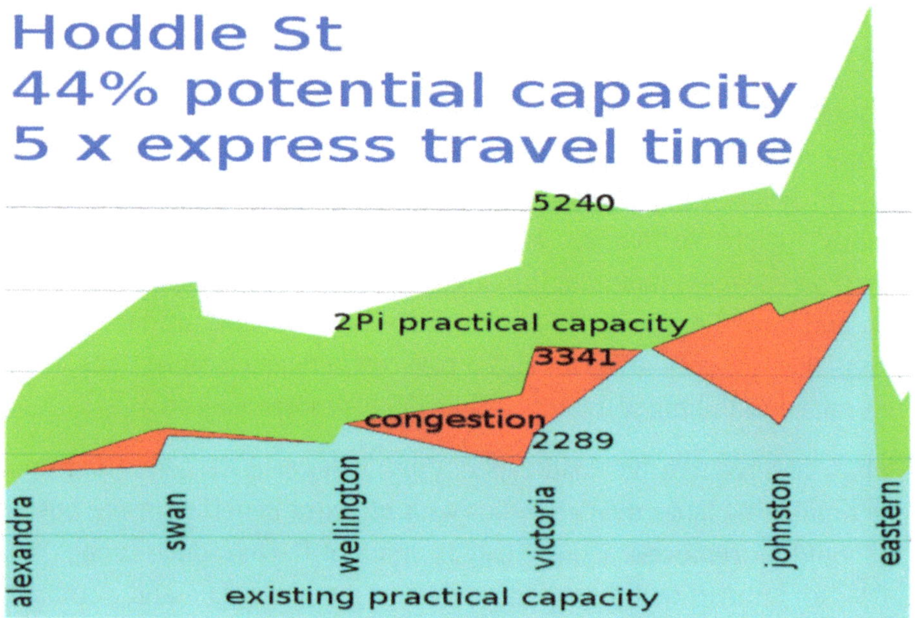

It is customary to model traffic capacity for intersections using the program Sidra and to compare the highest recorded traffic volumes from the SCATS signal records. Sidra computes the "practical" capacity, that is the highest traffic volume where free flow can be expected, as 90% of absolute congested capacity. The diagram shows the southbound AM peak capacities for all of the Hoddle St - Punt Rd route. Victoria St-Hoddle St is the most critical bottle-neck.

Meter Traffic, Link Signals and Smooth Flow.

The purpose of metering is to prevent congestion. Operation of Hoddle St and Punt Rd should be improved to produce a green wave, where a **platoon of traffic flows through sequential sets of traffic signals at**

the speed limit, in a compact bunch without dispersing, with the minimum of wasted time, braking, acceleration, and emissions. This would be at **practical capacity** for the critical intersection, being **90%** of absolute capacity at Victoria St. Signals at Victoria St count traffic, know when practical capacity is reached, and would tell the upstream signals when to turn red in order to gate or meter excess traffic. This message is passed back up the line to the Eastern Freeway, where vehicles may queue without reducing route capacity, at threat by the necessary reservation of a priority lane to jump the queue. The time gap between the traffic platoons will be relatively clear of traffic, allowing easier access to side streets and properties.

Having prevented congestion, signals along Hoddle St would be timed or linked towards Victoria St, being the peak direction, so that the platoon flows as smoothly as possible in a green wave. Linked signals must have the same cycle time so that the linking would repeat each cycle.

In the opposite or counter-peak direction, we are stuck with the peak direction timing, that may cause frequent disruption to the flow. Some smoothing counter-peak should be done at minor crossings by timing signals independently for each direction. So **pedestrian crossings need to be staged and minor streets converted to "left turn out only"** to smooth traffic flow in the counter-peak direction, reducing the number of stops and the CO2 emissions.

Then the outcomes are: minimums of trip time, CO2, and particulates; a reduction in associated noise; and easier access; that would all greatly improve the amenity of arterial streets. Congestion anywhere should never be permitted to occur, on the basis that the time it wastes is more costly than the alternatives. Congestion can best be removed by metering, that is much better than road pricing. Metering was successful for the Melbourne Commonwealth Games,

Two-phase, no turn arrows, cross-overs on all approaches, radical capacity increase

Installing two-phase intersections on a four-lane road gives it the capacity of a six-lane road. **Consideration for the customer can not lead to processing right turns in series** with the through flows at the intersection when the intersection is the critical constraint, not to mention that it is quite dangerous as has been proven in Utah, and liability attaches. This basic but radical fact was known to our brightest minds yet they have failed to act on it, world wide! Every intersection turn arrow is wasting people's time, including arrows on the cross road.

The queue delay on the Eastern Freeway is controlled by the capacity of the bottle-neck at Victoria St. If this bottle-neck is made worse by gating traffic, an extra 10% of traffic per hour will be delayed and all traffic will have to wait 10% of an hour longer in the queue, so capacity is very important. The best option **increases capacity by 70%**, by processing the right turn conflicts on all intersection approaches, **in parallel with the cross traffic**, instead of in series at the intersection, to create a "two-phase" intersection. A second immediate but inconvenient way to increase capacity by about 30% is to ban a pair of turns at the critical intersection. Drivers could turn left, then U-turn, or even find an alternative route of the same length instead. A third way that would increase capacity by 33% is to remove the bus lane that is no longer required, since there are free flow conditions for the bus. The bus should stop in the through lane for ease of operation. The number of intersections converted to two-phase operation should be a key performance indicator.

A further benefit of two-phase intersections is that signal cycle times can be reduced from the current 160 seconds to 60 seconds, reducing delays to all modes. **Both bus lane removal and two-phase intersections are extremely desirable.**

Queue Jumping, choose queue delay or 90% jump the queue for a small toll

It is highly desirable for most traffic to jump the queue because of the obvious time saving but also because that would save fuel and cut emissions. Additional lanes, toll gantries and lanterns for the priority traffic would be required. A new priority lane should be installed on the north approach to the freeway, on the basis that **provision should be made for priority traffic at all major queues**, including at freeway ramp meters. The proportion of traffic jumping major queues should be a key performance indicator as should the amount of delay at major queues to priority (all) traffic.

Currently the freeway shoulder is marked as a priority lane to be used by buses and government cars to jump the queue leading to Hoddle St, and it is controlled by a separate signal lantern. Highly valued trips made by community and business leaders, tradesmen, sales and deliveries are best made by private transport and constitute the most important and greatest quantity of traffic. They can not be avoided nor shifted to other modes without loss of value and they must be taken during the peak period. These trips warrant priority. Most vehicles now have e-tags so it is practical to toll the priority lane and permit all traffic to choose whether to enter the green wave via the queue or to pay a toll and enter via the priority lane(s). The **free entry option should be retained**, unlike the usual road pricing practice and the **price must be set so low as to attract 90%** of traffic, avoiding over-charging and minimising waste of time. There would be a relatively small increase to the queue delay.

Outcomes - The Impact of Metering, Two-phase Intersections and Queue Jumping

The following bar chart compares the existing state, with being metered, implying removal of the bus lane and installing a green wave, then with the added conversion of all seven major intersections to two-phase, and finally with the further added queue jumping.

The critical **capacity** shown in **green** at Victoria St is 3,300vph now, it increases to 4,500vph with removal of the bus lane, and increases further to 5,200vph with the addition of two-phase intersections.

The **trip time** shown in **blue** from the Yarra River at Alphington to the Yarra River at Cremorne is currently 40 minutes, it reduces to 25 minutes with removal of the bus lane, reduces further to 16 minutes with the addition of two-phase intersections, and finally reduces to 8 minutes for the 90% of express traffic that jumps the queue, but increases to 23 minutes for the 10% of queued free entry traffic.

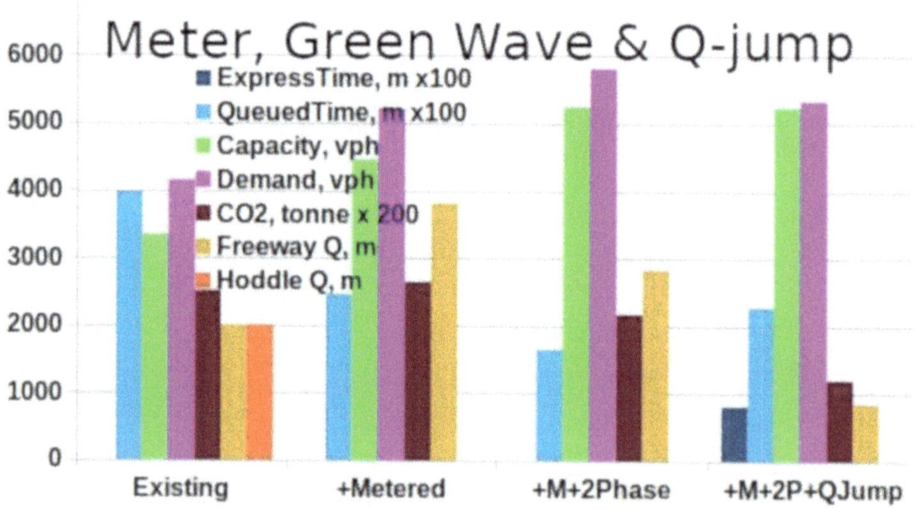

Because of the reduction of trip time, people get off the bus and back into their cars, so the **demand** shown in **magenta** that is now 4,200vph, increases to 5,300vph with removal of the bus lane, increases to 5,800vph with the addition of two-phase intersections, but then decreases to 5,400vph with the option of queue jumping. Note that a current capacity of 3,300vph and a current demand of 4,200vph means that 900 vph are added to the queue on the freeway. Also note that the queue delay increased by 7 minutes for the 520vph (10% of capacity) choosing not to pay the toll and that constrains demand down to

5,400vph. They may well be part of the 1,200vph for people that currently ride the bus but have switched to cars.

Emissions are strongly related to average trip time. CO2 **emissions** shown in **brown** are currently 12.5tonne/hr, they increase to 13.2tonne/hr with removal of the bus lane, reduce to 10.8tonne/hr with the addition of two-phase intersections, and reduce to only 5.9tonne/hr with queue jumping. Despite the much lower traffic volume, emissions for the existing traffic are only slightly lower because of the current slower trip speed. But queue jumping, by 90% of traffic when metered, drops CO2 emissions by an astonishing 53%! Jumping the queue is more important for emissions than capacity.

Currently the queues build to 2,000m on Hoddle St and spill back by 2,000m onto the Eastern Freeway. After metering, there will be no queues on Hoddle St, but 3,800m queues on the Eastern Freeway, reducing to 2,800m with the addition of two-phase intersections, and further reducing to a slow moving 800m queue with queue jumping.

Conclusion, lose all congestion, lose bus lanes, lose turn arrows, jump for a very low toll
Take Away: Find competent traffic engineers who can (a) replace all congestion with green waves, (b) convert all critical intersections to two-phase, and (c) install priority lanes with queue jump options for 90% of traffic at all queues.

Bus lanes should be removed and metering and signal linking immediately installed to better benefit the bus. Signals at minor streets and pedestrian crossings should be independently linked in each direction, requiring minor works. Two-phase intersections should be installed at seven intersections along the route, starting with Victoria St, enabling increased capacity so reduced queue length and delay, but also reducing delays to counter-peak traffic and to other modes. A priority lane should be installed from the north, possibly by extending the metering northwards to avoid reducing capacity. Toll gantries should be installed over priority lanes and all traffic given the choice of entry via a queue or priority entry via a small toll. The toll might be $1.50 to save 15 minutes after a two-phase intersection is installed at Victoria St. Until then, the delay for the 10% free access vehicles would be 46 minutes, not 23 minutes and the toll might need to be $3, saving 38 minutes, instead of the $1.50.

Arterials, no congestion, no turn arrows, jump queues for all arterials, customer focus

Serious consideration should be given to the reasons why public institutions world wide do not give enough priority to their customers. Green waves, two-phase intersections and queue jumping should be managed and reported by the traffic control room as key performance indicators, but under the umbrella of the ABS. For good governance, the reader will get the point about Governments not being trusted to report upon themselves. The existing outcome of neglect is hard to deny. The State department should report on KPI's for sites or routes nominated by each municipality, to keep the customer focus.

A suitable policy might include private enterprise traffic operations teams, charged with replacement of all congestion with metered lengths and green waves, enhanced in steps by smoothing minor crossings, two-phase intersections, and tolled queue-jumping. They should be tasked with publishing the strategy for each route, with costings, target dates and KPI's for each step. We might start with Hoddle St-Punt Rd and follow up with Alexandra Pde-Elliott Ave. A green wave is particularly relevant during every construction phase.

All congestion should be prevented and green waves implemented in the peak direction. Off-peak, pairs of arterials should be linked in opposite directions, for example Maroondah Hwy inbound and Canterbury Rd outbound, because the linked direction is much smoother and faster. Two-phase intersections, priority lanes and queue jumping should also be implemented, where congestion currently exists.

Freeways, no flow breakdown, queue jump at ramp meters, diverging diamonds at interchanges

Regular operation without breakdown during peak periods is highly desirable. The ramp metering should probably be more stringent to achieve fewer breakdowns but the problem needs much deeper insight. It is worthy of a separate investigation.

A secondary issue is that ramp meter queues are excessive, getting worse and indiscriminate. **Tolled priority lanes** would be self enforcing and should be **installed at all ramp meters**. Priority lanes at ramp meters have previously been tried for trucks but failed because of lack of compliance.

Another secondary issue is that conventional interchanges, including the single point interchange **should be replaced by "Diverging Diamond"** interchanges, that are the interchange version of a two-phase intersection. Diverging diamond interchanges reduce delay 24/7 and increase freeway capacity where the exit ramp is a constraint.

Freeway interchanges have 200% green time compared to 53% green time for existing intersections so interchanges are not critical and lane changing becomes the main concern. Freeway demand is already well managed by ramp metering but there are options for improvement. Of prime importance is the prevention of traffic incidents associated with lane changing but this requires more investigation and is not covered here.

DDI, Diverging Diamond Interchange, no turn arrows

A Diverging Diamond Interchange (DDI) is where arterial flows cross to the wrong side of the road, over the structure, and then cross back again. This is the preferred interchange option. It enables flows from both directions to enter the entry ramps by simply diverging without further signal control, except for ramp metering and pedestrian crossings, and also allows flows from the exit ramps to enter the arterial road, signalised in parallel with one of the arterial road through flows, or by added lanes. Pedestrians and cyclists should normally cross the structure in the centre, as shown here in blue, between protective barriers.

This sketch is overlaid on the Eastern Fwy - Hoddle St interchange and is a **pair of 2-phase intersections**. North is rotated to the right. Note the quite short clearance distances. A simulation[1] of this DDI option at the Eastern Fwy - Hoddle St interchange is shown on Youtube.

Many Pages of Supporting Details

Remove bus-lane, prevent congestion, link signals, smooth flow

To avoid congestion-delay to buses in Hoddle St, a bus lane has been reserved for them, reducing the capacity available to general traffic to 75% of its previous value. The bus lane has been very effective in removing delay to buses, but its side effect is an increase in the AM peak period delay by 15 minutes for 5,300 cars per hour, causing, 1,100 drivers to shift away from cars, mainly onto the bus, reducing the demand to 4,200 cars per hour, the existing state. While the existing bus lane removes congestion-delay to buses, that benefit could also have come from metering. The green wave and smoothing at minor crossings with metering would also remove delays to buses caused by traffic signals, so **metering is of greater benefit to buses** than a bus lane. Smoothing is presented later.

In Hoddle St, modelling shows that 1,100 people chose to use the bus rather than cop the extra 15 minutes delay. It follows that buses were available to substitute for 20% of trips, and that 20% of people prefer to take the bus than to endure the congestion. That is their decision to make, and it is based on their low value of the cost of mode change. But getting rid of congestion can: save 90% of people an average of 15 minutes each; improve amenity for residents; and with queue jumping reduce CO2 emissions by 53%. This is a demonstrated net benefit that would apply to some degree for all congested arterial streets. So to get rid of all congestion, anywhere, through metering, that need have no negative impact on capacity, net benefits apply, and the benefits of green waves would apply for all vehicles, including buses. **This thesis rejects the current practice of permitting congestion and installing a bus lane.**

A bus lane was installed in Stud Rd, where there were only 5 buses per hour, and reduced its capacity by 33%. This created huge delays for the general traffic, and caused such a public reaction, that it had to be removed. A similar response is expected for the 3-lane section of Hoddle St and in the 3-lane Punt Rd section of the route, where there are only 5 buses per hour, and such a proposal would reduce the capacity of the road by 33%. But **metering should be installed** there on the basis of removing congestion, with the benefit of also providing priority for buses. Metering is simply using traffic signals to prevent congestion, and reduce emissions and trip time. All traffic can use any lane. Metering creates or retains a queue.

Where there is no existing bus lane, **capacity should be maintained** preferably by installing two phase intersections or temporarily by banning right turns at the critical intersection(s).

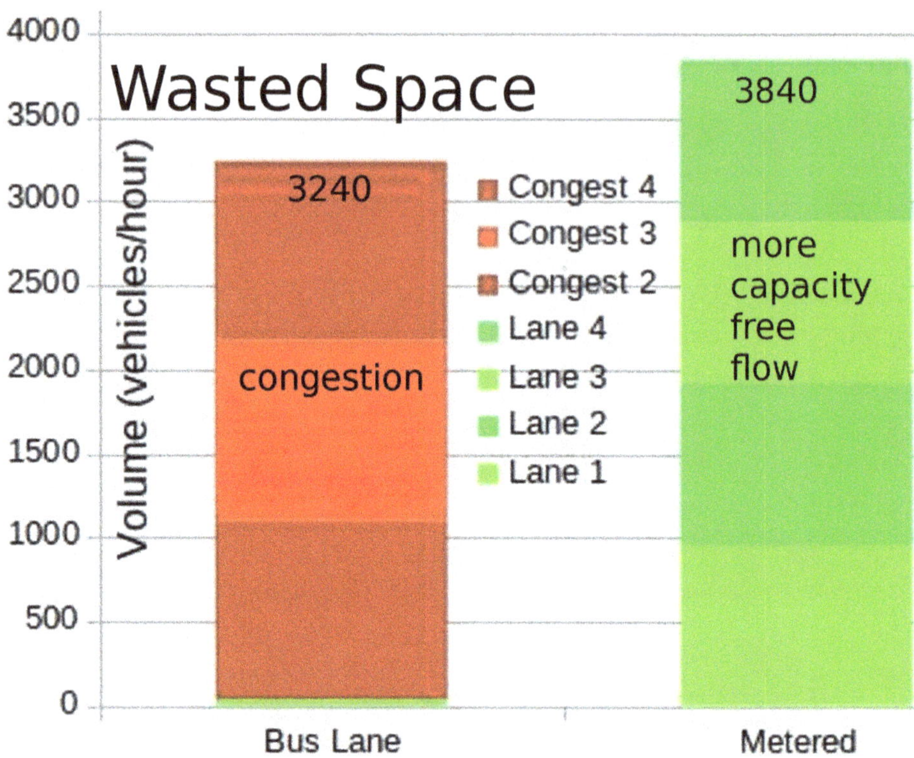

The figure compares the capacity for a 4-lane approach in Hoddle St, Melbourne: (a) with a bus lane and 3 congested lanes; and (b) a metered 4-lane approach without a bus lane. For the 4 metered lanes, a green wave can be applied, and the total capacity is 3,840 vehicles per hour. For one bus lane and 3 congested lanes, the buses have no congestion, but do not get a green wave, general traffic is highly congested, and the total capacity is only 3,240 vehicles per hour.

Meter, provide 10% spare downstream

The next figure illustrates the process of metering where traffic volumes entering the length are limited by the upstream signals. The traffic signal system records each vehicle at the stop line, noting the time gap between vehicles. Spare capacity is calculated at the downstream intersection and used to limit the flow at the upstream intersection. The objective is to **provide spare capacity of 3 right and 7 through** at

Victoria Pde. This 10% spare capacity requirement only applies to the critical intersection in a control group. Less critical intersections will require greater spare capacity, governed by an intersection further downstream. The simplest control is just of the 81 in the figure.

But a platoon will disperse because traffic is variable, so the faster drivers then learn that they are held up by red lights and the slower drivers will miss the end of the green and learn to keep up. The traffic engineer needs to remove any obvious causes of turbulence, such as lane changing, and then the signals engineer adjusts the time offset between signals to keep the platoon flow as lumpy as possible. This will be near the speed limit. Drivers should be advised of the ideal travel speed.

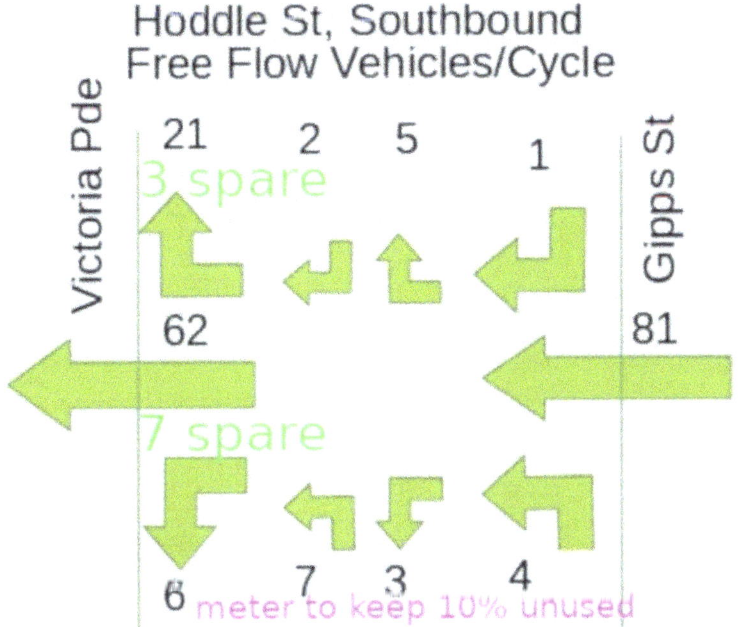

Easier access and shorter trip times will make trips by car more attractive, and they will increase in number, including from sources in the Hoddle St vicinity. So when the 1, 4, 2 & 7 in the figure grow significantly, they may also need to be constrained. Options are to meter them, to toll them, or ban them completely, or by time of day. Such moderation requires **endless maintenance**. The growth just doesn't impact the flows, it also impacts car ownership and parking availability.

If 3 right spare to the city can not be achieved by metering, and right turn queues block the through lanes, **a city entry toll** for right turns to the city at Victoria St may be required, perhaps for the whole morning peak, but free entry to the city would still be available via a right turn at Langridge St, Gipps St, Johnston St, or even Albert St. The only requirement here is that the intersection at Victoria St is not congested.

It has long been held that practical capacity is 90% of absolute capacity and that has been adopted here. The need to meter to exactly 90% of capacity can be modified empirically by adjusting the metering until it produces a satisfactory green wave, trading off higher capacity against smoother flow.

Link, note avoidable delays at minor crossings

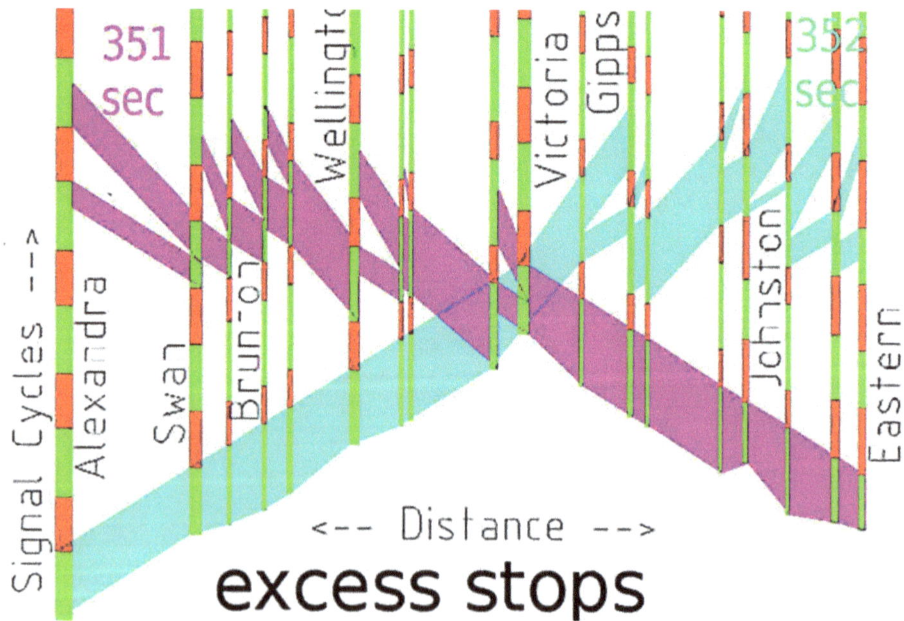

When there is metering, traffic signals will be linked for a green wave. These two diagrams show the progress of one platoon of traffic from each end of the Hoddle St route, nominally at the speed limit, but managed to provide a smooth flow for the peak traffic. The second diagram has flow **smoothed for the counter-peak direction** but the first diagram does not. The direction with the highest flow gets priority and so defines the relative signal timing between intersections. Observe the smooth flow from each end towards Victoria St in the AM peak. This sets the timing for signals in the other, counter-peak, directions. All the signals must operate with the same cycle length so that the same timing happens next cycle.

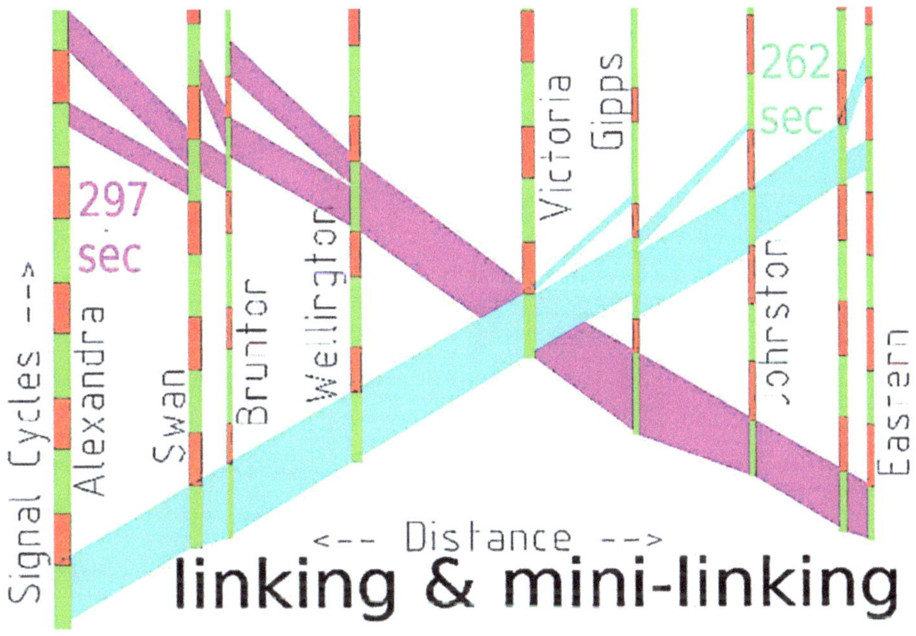

Only one platoon of traffic is shown in each direction for clarity. The diagrams have been drawn with 60 second signal cycle time that is only possible with two-phase intersections. Had they been drawn with the current 160 second cycle time, delays in the counter-peak components, beyond Victoria St would have been much greater.

Once traffic passes Victoria St, it is running counter-peak and some, or all of it, is delayed by minor intersections or pedestrian signals. Where delays caused to the counter-peak flow, exceed potential delays to pedestrians if they were to be staged, and delays to minor flows if they were to turn left and then U-turn, **smoothing flow is justified**.

Average travel time is 6 minutes each way for the Excess Stops figure, compared to 4-5 minutes with perfect linking between major intersections in the Linking & Mini-Linking figure.

Note that this example only uses signals that have the same cycle time. It may be necessary to have a discontinuity between lengths of route with different cycle times.

Smoothing Detail. Common practice on major arterial streets to avoid disruptions to the flow by minor crossings, is to **not have a median break opposite side streets**, and to have U-turn breaks elsewhere. Pedestrian crossings are staged. Alternatively, a Restricted Crossing, U-turn layout as shown, is provided.

Converting minor intersections to "left-in, left-out, right-in", also known as "Restricted Crossing, U-turn", and staging pedestrian crossings, allows independent timing of the signals for each direction. Although the time savings is small, the experience of many stops over a short distance is frustrating, energy consuming, increases emissions, and applies for all modes.

Where median breaks exist at minor streets, the right turns from the major road can be retained, but the **straight across and right turns from the minor streets need to be re-directed**. With the arrangement shown, linking for southbound traffic, fixes timing of left-in, left-out and right-in to Elizabeth St, on the right, and of pedestrians and cyclists crossing southbound traffic. Timing is different for northbound linking, that controls left-in, left-out and right-in to Albert St, and of pedestrians and cyclists crossing northbound traffic. U-turn opportunities may need to be provided in Hoddle St to replace the right turns and straight across for the traffic from the minor streets .

History, faltering steps to removing turn arrows

Existing intersections, particularly those operating in excess of 90% capacity, can be converted to two-phase, **within the existing footprint with capacity and delay benefits as well as safety**. This conclusion is widely applicable because because it was **tested on 30 of the most difficult sites**. They were sketched and modelled in detail to retro-fit 2Pi within their existing footprint and the result was a vast improvement in capacity, delay and alignment for each of them. Further, in contrast to the conventional bias towards increasing the footprint size, all the designs tested for this concept used the existing footprint, existing number of lanes and lane widths, and still achieved a major increase in capacity with better alignments than existing, and increased safety.

"Continuous flow" intersections are used in Utah on the Bangerter Highway. They have cross-overs on the main approaches to the intersections, but not on the side road approaches. Federal funding is limited to the highway approaches. Turn conflicts with opposing traffic are resolved on the main approaches with a "cross-over", saving time lost at the intersection due to one turn phase. These intersections have ~35% improvement in capacity and delay and ~50% improvement in safety. Cross-overs are presented shortly.

Common sense will tell you that the delays caused by turn conflicts from the side road are of similar size and should also be removed, although this has not been done before. It can fit within the existing footprint, and is more **driver friendly** if all approaches are the same. There are different ways to resolve the right turn conflict, but the essential requirement is for the intersection to have only two signal phases, and it should be known as such, a "two-phase" intersection.

Cross-overs for Utah's "**Continuous flow**" intersections are positioned at a distance from the cross road such that the right turners only stop once, so the right turners have continuous flow. This places the cross-over ~200m from the cross road. This is **unsuitable for the urban context** with access to properties; for short flaring; does not have the option of multiple cross-overs; gives undue importance to the right turns; some drivers miss their turns; yet the proposed two-phase intersections do not have these problems.

Increasing capacity improves the quality of service by reducing the delay at an intersection queue. In fully developed urban areas, it can be quite disruptive to acquire property to widen the road reserve. So it is highly desirable to get the most traffic capacity out of the existing number of traffic lanes. Approaches to major intersections often have short additional lanes, known as flaring, but to match the mid-block capacity, that would need to double the number of through lanes, and to have full utilisation of those extra lanes. Most flaring lanes are usually reserved to safeguard turning traffic, with its differential speed.

In addition to flaring, a good strategy is to install a two-phase intersection, (2Pi), and to resolve right turn conflicts with the opposing through traffic on the approaches, **within the flaring**, timed to coincide with the cross traffic. This might require an additional set of traffic signals on each approach, but they are easily justified on the basis of a 70% increase in capacity, safer operation, lower delays, avoidance of property acquisition, better lane utilisation, and less turbulence. For prudence, these signals would only be required on the basis of traffic engineering analysis.

Two phase intersections are also called parallel flow intersections, continuous flow intersections, displaced right turns, or displaced left turns, but the descriptions are often inconsistent for the concept being used.

2-phase Intersections, extra capacity, better safety, reduced delay

Instead of sitting on the approach, doing nothing while the cross traffic runs, the right turners perform a "get-out-of-the-way" movement, by crossing the path of the opposing through traffic, thereby operating in parallel with the intersection cross traffic and **avoiding the delay of a separate turn phase at the intersection**. Separating these right turn conflicts away from the intersection simplifies driving decisions, and has an enormous benefit for safety, with only half the crashes, so **all conventional intersections are now relatively dangerous**, and should no longer be built on the bases of safety, capacity and delay.

The figure "Wasting Time" compares the allocation of time for the conventional 4-phase and the proposed 2-phase intersections, both with 120 second cycles. In practice, 4-phase intersections often need 120 second cycle times in order to limit the proportion of lost time: amber and all red. Longer cycle time increases capacity at the expense of delay. With 2-phase intersections they have no turn phases at the intersection, and capacity is increased by 69% for 120 second cycles, calculated from 90/53. But for the current proportion of lost time, 2-phase intersections should normally operate with **60 second cycles** with only **51% more capacity** and importantly, **much less delay**. Maximum delay for through cars is then one short phase of 36 seconds for 2-phase intersections, instead of 3 longer phases for 94 seconds for 4-phase intersections. The option of operating the 2-phase intersection at 120 second cycles with greater capacity is retained.

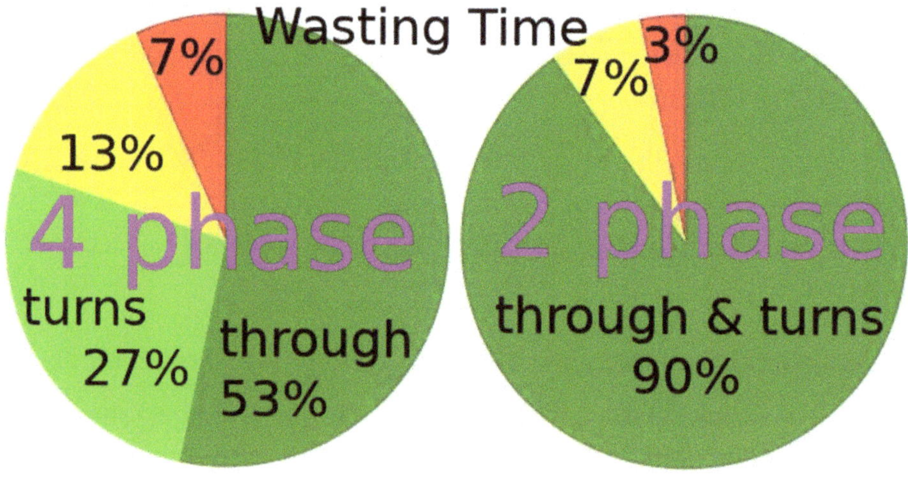

A simulation[1] of the Victoria St - Hoddle St intersection is shown on Youtube using 5,240vph southbound. It has a green wave, no residual queues and carries 57% more than the existing congested intersection that has a volume of only 3,341vph southbound and 4km of queue, extending past four more intersections and on to the Eastern Freeway. If queue jumping is permitted, average trip time is then 9 minutes instead of the current 40 minutes.

Complex intersections with more than four legs can, and should be **converted to four legs**, where 2-phase intersections can be applied. A simulation[1] of a 2-phase intersection with six approaches at Princes Hwy - Springvale Rd - Centre Rd is on Youtube, although this intersection warrants a grade separation.

The safety, delay and capacity benefits of processing right turns on approaches should also apply for low volume un-signalised intersections.

Crossover, driver friendly, direct short cut, within existing footprint

A cross-over is a more **driver friendly** and much preferred option because the right turner **enters the turn lane at the same location** as usual; turners pass through the intersection only once; and the turn alignment looks, and is, a **short cut** with a better than normal alignment. This is particularly advantageous for **trucks** and at intersections with **acute** angles where split phases are currently necessary, because opposing turns cannot turn at once as a result of the geometry, so through and right from one direction then have to proceed together, less efficiently. The conflicting movements at cross-overs are simpler, slower and safer.

Note that the right turn lane(s) cross to a right hand service road half way towards the intersection, usually under signal control; and the alignment of the opposing through movement forms a plait with the right turn lane, **staying within the current intersection footprint**. The opposing through flow has high alignment standards. The right turn has sharper curves yet low off-tracking of 10cm if the turn radii are at least 30m. The right turners potentially queue twice but since the cycle time is shorter, the required total storage length is about the same, so intersection flaring does not need to be lengthened.

The simulation[1] of Victoria St - Hoddle St shows cross-overs on the north and west approaches. A cross-over only interrupts one carriageway, so signals can be perfectly timed to link with the main intersection, and not disrupt the through movements. The right turners then cross in the shadow of the cross street operation. As shown in the simulation, signal timing often means that turners are not stopped at the second stop line, (it is continuous flow by chance).

Triple Crossover, saves time if the right turn is heavy

A triple cross-over is shown here is on the Hoddle St north approach so that a **heavy right turn** does not wastefully increase the phase time for the combined cross-over and Victoria St. The figure is rotated with north to the right. There is a heavy right turn from Hoddle St, with 40 seconds green, into Victoria St, with 10 seconds green. The turners have

10 seconds, and **6 lanes provided** to cross the opposing Hoddle St through lanes, but only 2 lanes are needed to complete the turn into Victoria St at the main intersection, during the 40 seconds, and before the early cut off. Multiple cross-overs mean that turns are not critical for maximum capacity.

Pedestrians, shorter, faster, safer crossings with clear channels, fortuitous timing

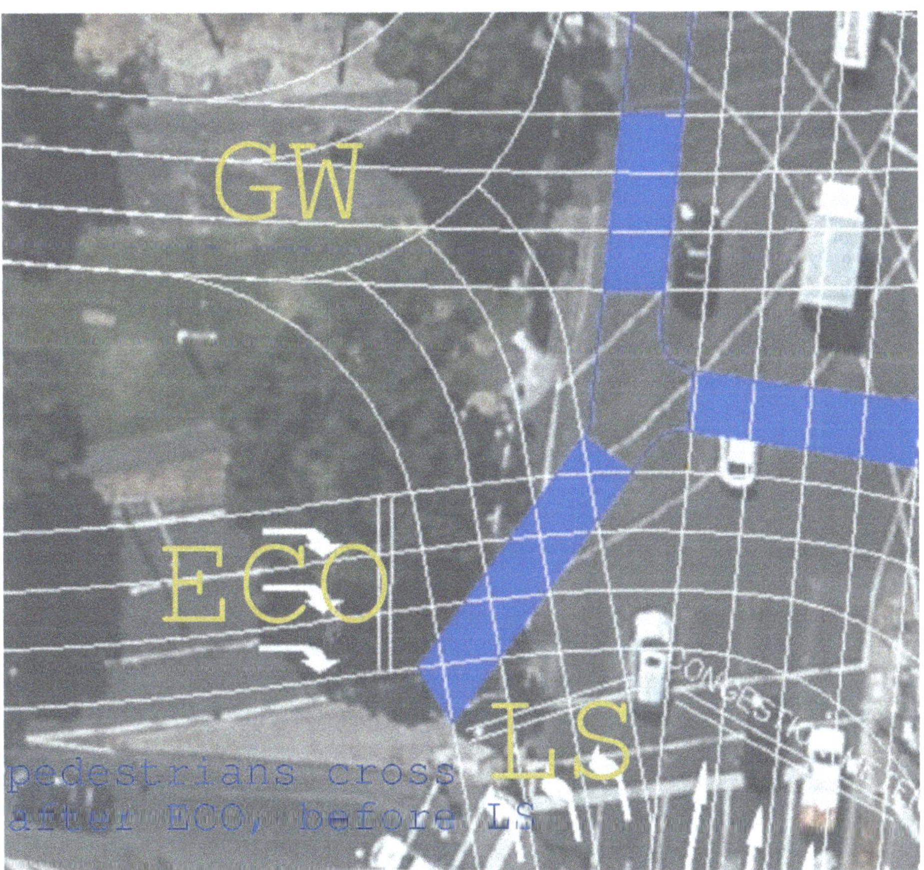

Full signal control of all turns in slip lanes has better pedestrian and cyclist safety. Pedestrian crossings are shown in blue. Right turns would have an early cut-off, "ECO" and left turns a late start, "LS" to enforce sharing of the phase time in the road being entered. With both left and right turns in the same slip lane and under full signal control, pedestrians and cyclists in their own sub-phase, can then cross **after the ECO from one approach and before the LS from the adjacent approach**, without any impact on capacity and with greater safety.

This full **signal control of pedestrians and clear channels for vehicles** is safer than filtering right and left turners through pedestrians. The lower cycle times of 2-phase intersections, and staged crossings reduce delay to pedestrians and other modes, assisting compliance. Pedestrians cross fewer lanes than for conventional intersections. So that right turners are never stranded across through lanes at the end of the phase, right turns, from up the page, are signed with a give way for the left turn, from down the page, where they join the departure, labelled "GW", because they are in the same phase. **Line-marking similar to a roundabout** as shown reinforces the priority.

P-turn, uncertainty to be avoided

Indirect turns are **inefficient and confusing**. Right turners in a P-turn: go through, perform a U-turn and then a left turn, as is shown in magenta on this sketch of Victoria St - Hoddle St. P-turn is to be firmly avoided because it is unusual; needs to be signed in advance; leaves open the option for people to turn right, illegally and unsafely, where they conventionally do; and incurs extra travel distance.

Q-turn,. counter intuitive to be avoided

Indirect turns are **inefficient and confusing**. Right turners in a Q-turn: turn left, then perform a U-turn, as is shown in green on this sketch of Victoria St - Hoddle St. Q-turn is to be firmly avoided because it is unusual; must be performed from the left; needs to be signed in advance; and incurs extra travel distance. A Q-turn has been used at Moorooduc Hwy - Cranbourne Rd intersection.

Only the cross-over option is driver-friendly.

Regarding this sketch, having two-phase intersections, 2Pi, is critical for capacity and delay. On the south approach, the 100 vehicles per hour right turn lane is replaced with a Q turn, shown green, to gain an extra through lane within a restricted footprint, a gain of 1,000vph. On the east approach, the right turn is replaced with a P turn, shown magenta, to prevent queuing on the tram track. These P-turn and Q-turn options with low volumes increase capacity even though traffic re-enters the intersection. The option of simply banning these two turns is worse because drivers could still make the same manoeuvres but without signing guidance and with longer detours. The option with the highest practical capacity, for the target pattern of traffic demand, will reduce delays. The existing layout for this intersection has a practical capacity of 2,289vph southbound; it is currently operated highly congested at 3,341vph; and the 2Pi design sketched has a practical capacity of 5,240vph. Sidra was used to calculate the practical capacities.

The simulation[1] of the Victoria St - Hoddle St intersection includes the P-turn and Q-turn on the sketch. While in theory, only two U-turns are needed to process four right turns at an intersection, and the example shows one U-turn serving two right turns, this should be firmly avoided because it is not driver friendly. It is only proposed here because it is such a critical intersection, and might save nominally 3,000vph 15 minutes each.

Parallel Flow, waste of space and disconcerting

This option is inferior to the other three options. Parallel flow, is a right turn from the conventional location, but into a near-side service road, during the side road phase, crossing back to the normal lanes some distance down the departure leg. This option uses right turn arrows from the main road when the cross traffic is running. A presentation of parallel flow is on Youtube. Either the cross back to the normal location interrupts both directions so can't be linked both ways to the main intersection, or the cross back is to an additional median lane, that then merges. Both require yet another lane for the left turn from the side road being entered, that must diverge before the cross back. Requiring additional lanes within a restricted footprint **seriously reduces capacity**. Parallel flow is used at Punt Rd-Olympic Bvd.

Continuous Left Turn, dangerous with hoons, disjointed for pedestrians

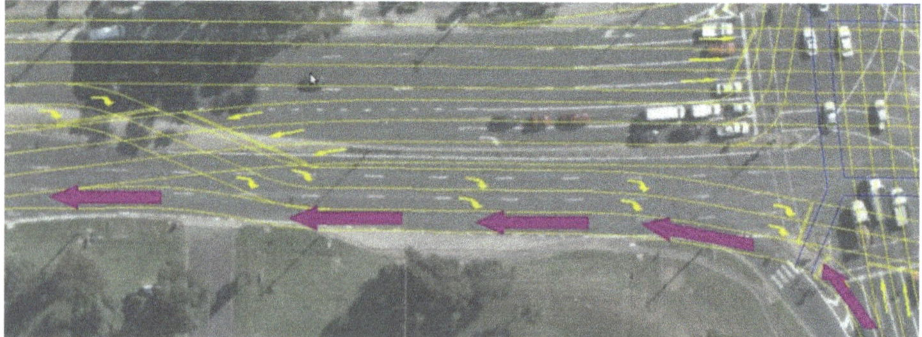

A continuous left turn for the length of the right turn service road, shown here in magenta, is **dangerous** because drivers run through the red signal too often at pedestrian crossings in continuous slip lanes, particularly when the turn radius is good and the speed is higher, and the lane is better used as an additional through lane or right turn lane. Prefer the arrangements shown previously, designed to improve pedestrian safety and increase capacity.

Unsafe Two-Phase Intersections, cheap and nasty

Intersections where right turns filter through opposing traffic and pedestrians, may have only two phases but filtering is relatively dangerous and is often done to maintain capacity on the cheap. They are literally two-phase but only because some conflicting movements **are not signal controlled as they should be**. Pedestrian safety is decreased by having vehicles filtering through pedestrians, and having more and longer pedestrian crossings than with full channelisation and full signalisation.

Queue Jump for all, not just the privileged few

Demand should always be constrained by delay at the metering queue. Some people constrained by this delay will take the bus. This delay wastes time for those caught in the queue and the queue increases the CO_2 emissions, both of which should be avoided to the greatest extent possible. People whose time is more valuable should be able to jump the queue and the best way to decide who and when that is warranted is to let the user decide with a toll. If the toll is set too high, less than 90% will jump the queue and some valuable trips will be delayed. **If the toll is set too low, all priority traffic will be delayed** by metering. It is difficult to set the toll to have the desired effect, so the toll needs to be flexible. 90% queue jumping drops the CO_2 emissions by ~53%.

This free entry queue is a buffer between the toll being too high and too low. The toll should be set so that priority traffic was rarely delayed, and the delay in the queue would then constrain the demand, but only if necessary to prevent congestion.

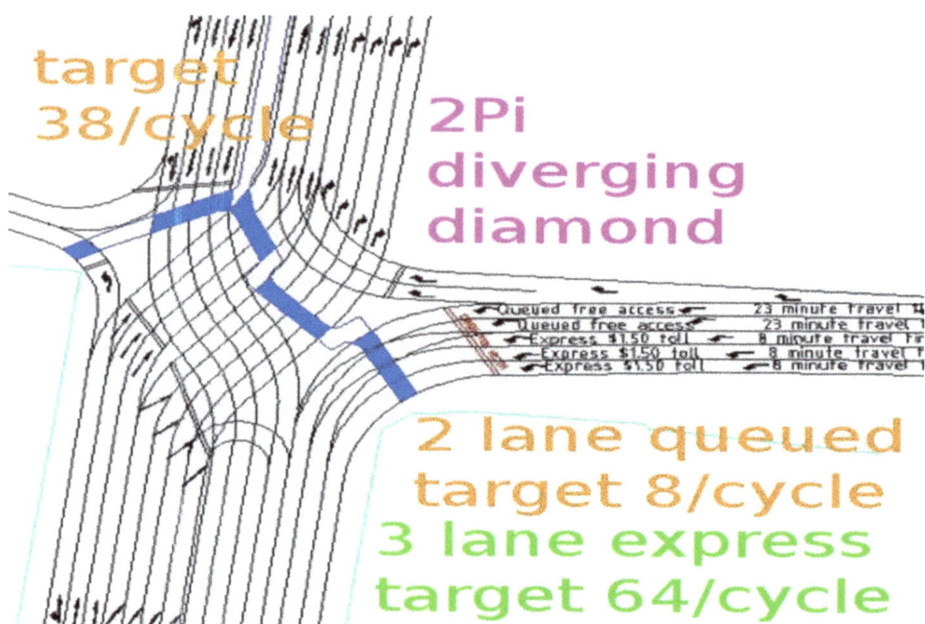

The conventional area pricing is coarser. If there was area pricing, a queue-jumping toll would still be required, unless the toll was overkill. Area pricing is less selective in toll location and so its constriction will reduce the level of service. It does not have as much equity and does not moderate local traffic within the cordon.

To overcome any political negatives, the toll should be installed for three months and then removed. Users should be polled to measure acceptance and if strongly endorsed, the tolled queue-jump reinstated. The southern half of a diverging diamond interchange of Hoddle St with the Eastern Fwy is shown. **Three lanes from the Eastern Fwy are proposed to be tolled and two retained for a free entry queue.** Priority lanes are not proposed in Hoddle St, south of the Eastern Fwy, just a green wave. Note that a new priority entry is also proposed from the north. The toll should be pitched low for maximum uptake, saving time, estimated at $1.50 to save 15 minutes, and reducing pollution.

If the trip via the queued lanes on the Eastern Fwy is reduced from 40 to 23 minutes, demand from the Eastern Fwy grows to 96 vehicles/cycle.

Metered capacity of Hoddle St is 110 v/c total, apportioned with 38 v/c from the north, and 72 v/c from Eastern Fwy. The Eastern Fwy toll is set so up to 64 v/c queue jump, and 8 v/c will be discharged from the queue. The excess of demand (96) over supply (72), 24 v/c, is added to the queue. If the toll is set too low, the priority lanes will be limited to 72 v/c by metering. If the toll is set too high, the balance of the 64 will be discharged from the queue. Metering combined with road pricing reduces trip time and emissions but we need also to retain the equity of free entry.

Metering prevents congestion but produces or retains a metering queue. The most critical intersection for the southbound traffic in Hoddle St is at Victoria St, but the metering must be cascaded through successive intersections to constrain the queue 2km upstream at the end of the Eastern Fwy, otherwise the queued lanes plus the lanes required for priority traffic will create a greater restriction.

Queue jumping is also known as congestion charging, FasTrak, and high occupancy toll (HOT) lanes and is a form of road pricing where there can be a variable toll. High occupancy lanes are not being proposed, just tolled priority jumping of the queue, as happens now for a privileged few for free. **User choice should at least be available for all**, rather than a select few, and it can cut emissions in half. Huge benefits would accrue to the community from faster trips, and there is still free access.

Proportion Jumping, more & more save time

For time efficiency, and low CO2, as many people as possible should get priority entry. The practical limit to this is probably 90%.

Assuming we have not yet installed two-phase at Victoria St, with no queue jumping except for the bus, all traffic takes 25 minutes. But if priority vehicles jump the queue and take only 8 minutes, for a toll, then modelling with 50%, 70% or 90% jumping, the free entry vehicles would take 41, 44, or 46 minutes respectively, demand would decrease from 5,300 to 5,100, 4,800, and 4,600 respectively, and the queue length would decrease significantly.

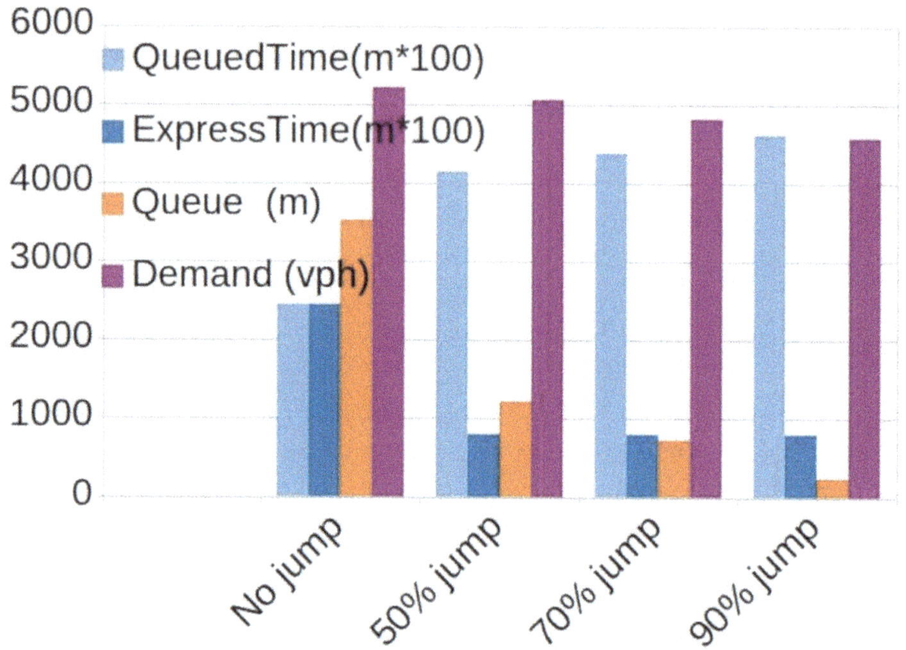

Average trip times for all traffic would be 25, 16, 13, and 10 minutes respectively, so 90% is the best outcome. Priority trip time drops from 25 minutes to 8 minutes with queue jumping, saving 17 minutes, but the free access queue trip time increases, with an apparent saving of 38 minutes for queue jumping, so the toll might have to be $3 while there is no 2Pi at Victoria St. The practical trade-off is between frequency of metering priority traffic and quantity of trip time saved.

Demand and Equity, reduce trip time and they come from the bus

With 2Pi at Victoria St, for tolled queue jumping, the free queue travel time for the trip increases by 7 minutes for 10% of traffic, and for the tolled 90% of traffic reduces by 8 minutes. This is a net benefit and it provides a **new express travel option for essential trips**. Note that there will still be 28% more trips, from mode change, than currently exist, but an additional 11% will have gone back to their previous mode.

This puts the queued 10% proposed to be used for demand management, into perspective. The target is a reliable 8 minutes, instead of the current 40 minutes.

Metering and two-phase intersections will increase capacity. Queues will clear quicker and travel times reduce. Then demand will increase by about 2% for each travel time minute saved. Because of metering and two-phase intersections, more and more mode change trips occur. Trips will be made by car instead of being on the bus, on bikes, by walking, made at other times, or not made at all. These mode change trips are of **low marginal value to the maker to be made by car**.

My bleeding heart says why should the poor people be subject to delay? But give me a break, these people are currently riding the bus.

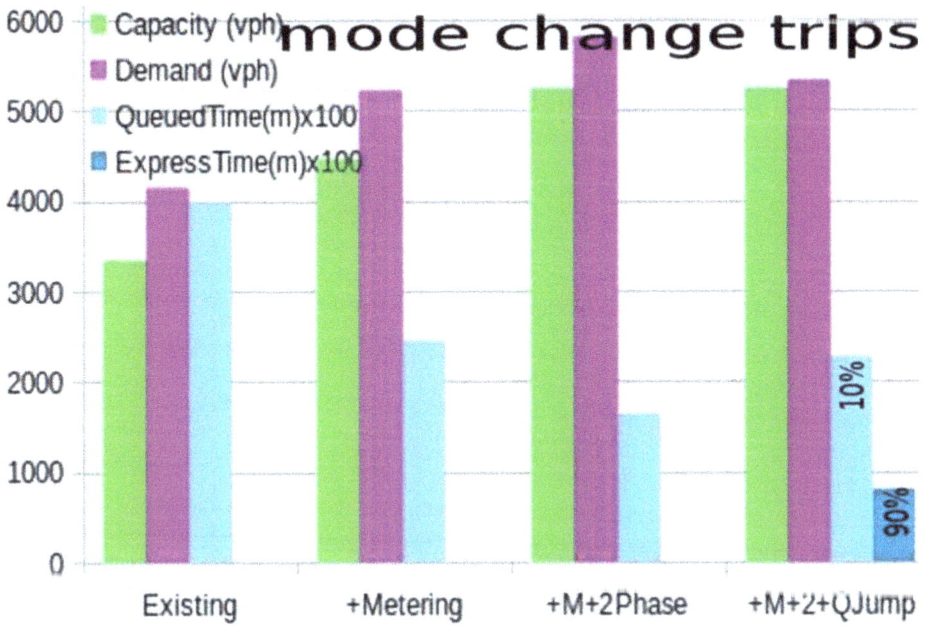

Path Grading Detail. Traffic islands must have kerbed cut-throughs for the vision impaired, as shown here, but use three full width tactile tiles and no internal tiles. It should have **flat, 2% grades** for self cleaning, not steep kerb ramps. All these improvements assist pedestrians, the vision-impaired, prams, wheelchairs, cyclists and traffic.

At major intersections, cyclists must be encouraged to mix with pedestrians rather than with car traffic, using wide cross-walks and cyclist lanterns.

Monash Single Point Interchange, heaps of lost time, lacks queue space & priority option

A Diverging Diamond Interchange, as sketched on top, would have a delay cost of only $5,012/hr compared to a delay cost of $11,115/hr for the existing single point interchange, for the same size footprint, using the existing structure. It would better accommodate ramp meter queues. Because of the much shorter clearance distances and fewer phases, the 2-phase DDI has: half the delay; twice the capacity; half the crashes; and fewer gridlocks, compared to a single point interchange.

Converting all freeway interchanges to diverging diamonds should be given serious consideration for safety, delay and capacity reasons.

Two lanes have been provided for the right turns to the ramp meters, **one of which should be a priority lane.** The single lane left turn to the ramp meter can be either a priority lane or not, but not both.

Where there are ramp meters, the meter can be at the top of the ramp, with queues extending through the structure. Ramp meters limit the flow of traffic to the freeway to avoid flow breakdown. Meters at the top of the ramp reduce the required ramp length, and increase the distance to the next freeway exit, so reducing freeway turbulence. A video for Marvin Rd interchange in Washington State reported 60 DDI's built since 2009, having greater capacity, with 50% crash reduction, and lower crash severity.

This single point interchange at Monash Fwy, Toorak Rd , previously considered efficient, and having only 3 phases, has **double the delay** of a diverging diamond interchange. Note the **long existing clearance**

distances, covering the width of the Freeway underneath, that cause considerable lost time with amber and all-red and these long clearances are more likely to **fail and be blocked**.

Freeway Operation, excess breakdown, needs priority toll, needs anti-swooping, needs lidar

Congestion on freeways leads to **flow breakdown**, loss of throughput, consequent increased delays, and **should never be permitted** by the control strategy, but this is not consistently achieved.

Ramp metering already makes provision for high priority vehicles to jump the entry queue, but it needs to be further developed to include a **priority toll**, as is proposed above for arterial streets, to permit as many vehicles as possible to jump the queue, where the **queue delay or queue length is significant**. Allowing 90% traffic to use the priority lane for a small toll, reduces the ramp meter queue length by 90%, increases the queue delay slightly for the 10% free entry queue, slightly reduces the demand, reduces the queue CO_2 emissions by 90%, and reduces the average delay by 90%. Both the priority and queued lanes need to be metered, but the priority lane should normally flow freely. This 90% reduction in queue length is important where the ramp meter queue is 1.5km long, and jumping is important when the queue delay is 30 minutes.

The need to prevent crashes is even more important for all safety, delay and reliability aspects. Contemporary understanding of freeway crashes is rapidly developing, and it is considered that two classes of freeway crash are prevalent: those at medium density, at moderate speed, associated with **lane changing with 0.3 second gaps**, with serious consequences, described as "swooping"; and those at high density, at low speed, with minor consequences, and described as "rear-end". Control systems seek to avoid occurrences of high densities and rear-ends. Regulation of swooping needs to be invented.

Limiting the exposure to swooping is restricted by sub-par observation equipment. Professor Boris Kerner has defined a 3-phase model of traffic flow that better explains observed traffic behaviour than the widely accepted two-phase model. Not to be confused, the two phase model of traffic flow relates to the speed, volume, and density of traffic flow; but two-phase operation of signals is the number of primary signal phases at an intersection. John Gaffney and Matthew Hall of VicRoads have observed freeway traffic behaving according to the 3-phase model, including nucleations, derived from TIRTL measurements at 500m intervals on the Monash Freeway and associated road crashes. Refer also to John Gaffney's Churchill Fellowship report.

Individual vehicle behaviour cannot be observed in detail from the TIRTL measurements. Better equipment to observe traffic behaviour is used by driver-less cars and should be used by the road operator for safety research and more generally for signal control. Jeff Hecht writes that: automotive lidar remains in flux; long-range microwave radar works better in bad weather; ultrasound is best for parking assist; short-medium range radar is good for cross traffic, rear-end collision and blind spot detection, optical cameras have good resolution and can detect traffic signals; and lidar can directly measure distance and speed for objects up to 300m. An example from Luminar lidar is shown, but it is likely that a combination of a few technologies can best observe traffic and will come from the car industry.

While the process described above is proposed to craft green waves on arterial roads, it has limited application for freeways. Melbourne's freeway and tollway network carries 30% of the arterial road traffic although comprising only 7% of the arterial road network length. Progress is being made on managing freeway operation to achieve optimum speed, without congestion, and to establish reliable trip times.

Ramp metering to control freeway traffic has proven successful as described in VicRoads' Freeway Ramp Metering Handbook. The method uses occupancy as a criterion to limit inflows and avoid congestion. Managing varying entry flows across adjoining ramps can spread the micro peaks, decrease freeway turbulence, and increase freeway capacity.

Speed control is used on freeways related to traffic incidents, including roadworks, and care is taken with the rate of change of speed and associated densities to avoid unsafe states. VicRoads practice is to reduce speeds in 10kph increments during incidents because of road safety. The Police practice of **stopping vehicles on freeways**, requiring a 60kph speed change increment has proven to be relatively **dangerous** and should be avoided. Better to direct offenders to an exit ramp.

It is necessary for Police to make safe accident sites on freeways, but the practice of **closing the road** for investigation beyond the time needed to clear the site, is excessive and **can not be justified**. Often the cause of the crash was not involved in the crash and has long departed.

Streamlining Hoddle Street.

The original proposal for Streamlining Hoddle St, for a total of $41.8M, was checked by Treasury. It included two-phase intersections for seven sites: Eastern Fwy, $6.9M; Victoria St, $6.5M; Johnston St, $3.8M; Wellington Pde, $6.2M; Swan St, $5.1M; Alexandra Ave, $2.8M; and Gipps St, $2.5M. Smoothing works, $7.0M, were proposed for Truro St, Langridge St, Albert St, Hotham St, Freeman St, Rowena Pde, and Richmond Tce. Albert St was the example for smoothing. A new connection to Brunton Ave, $2.0M was proposed.

VicRoads reviewed these designs and have implemented different concepts but only at three of the intersections, Eastern Freeway, Johnston Street and Swan Street/Olympic Boulevard, yet has not adopted the green wave concept requiring metering, nor smoothing flow at minor crossings, nor tolled queue jumping. The cost increased from the estimated $16M to $110M for the three intersections. There is little evidence that the Government's stated objective of improvements to the trip time along Hoddle St and Punt Rd were considered. Until the major constriction at **Victoria St has two-phases**, the capacity of the route will be unchanged. Current improvements will have inbuilt capacity constrictions that will then be tested. Unless **metering removes congestion**, express trips are not available. When **high priority queue jumping** is adopted, extensive queue delay and high CO2 emissions will reduce. The prescription is in this book. VicRoads have done **some road works for capacity but none of the improvements for trip time.**

Simulations[1] of the diverging diamond at Eastern Fwy-Hoddle St and simulations of the five two-phase intersections at Johnston St-Hoddle St, Victoria St-Hoddle St, Bridge Rd-Hoddle St, Punt Rd-Swan St, and Alexandra Ave-Punt Rd are on Youtube.

This sketch is of a two-phase intersection at Victoria St-Hoddle St and it incorporates many radical concepts.

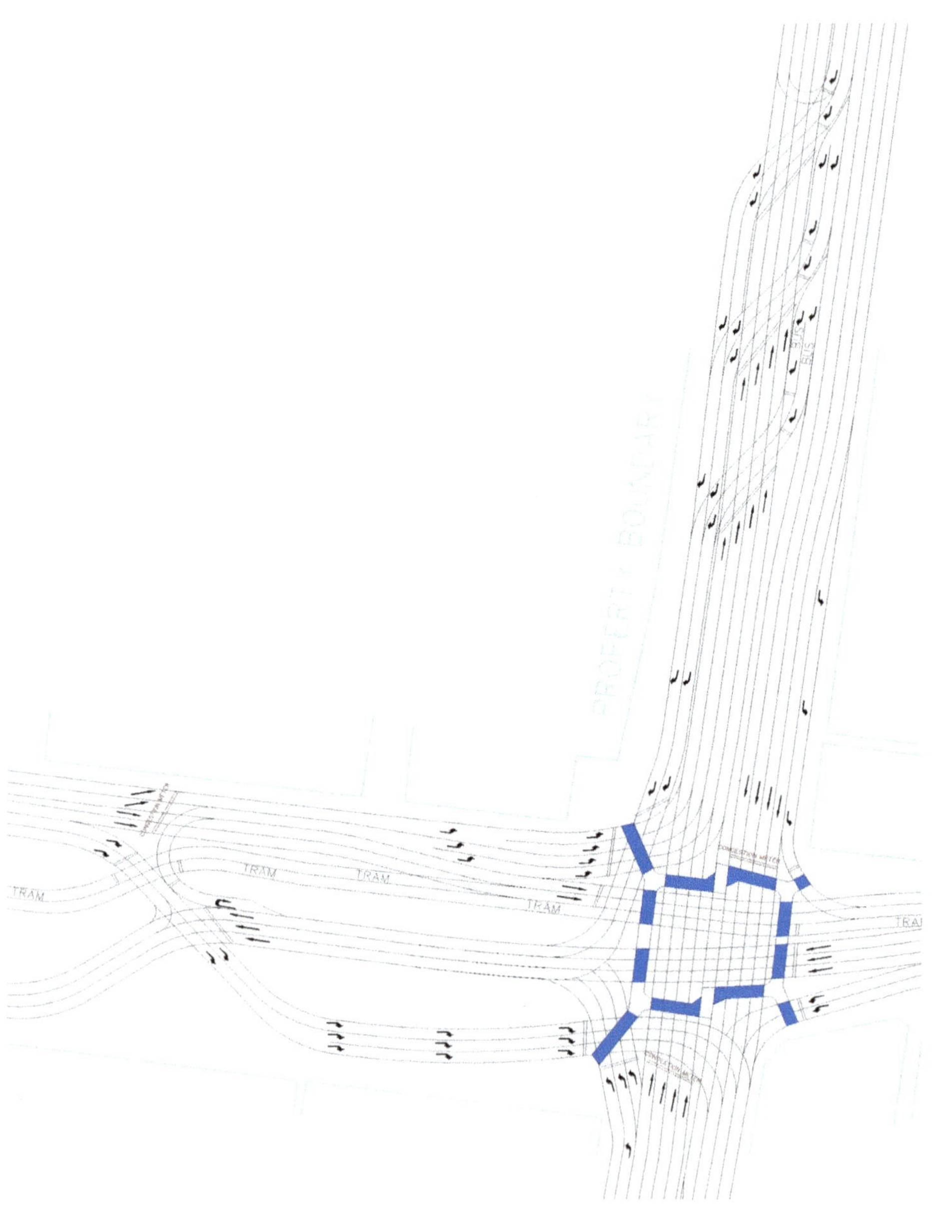

Aerial Podcars, 2021 Edition, Profitable, fast, reliable, cheap transport, better service than cars

Transport Proven Insipid, One Dynamic Solution, Benefits of Enterprise

Existing transport performance is insipid. Peak hour trips for cars only average 15kph, 23kph and 38kph, for the inner, middle and outer Melbourne areas. Similarly, trips for public transport only average 10kph, 18kph and 23kph. Comparing those trip times to 60kph for aerial podcars, the annual **delay cost would be $22B**, just for peak periods.

Externalities of transport systems are very serious problems. Cost recovery for public transport is only 22%, requiring subsidies. There are 3,000 hospitalised road casualties per year. The road toll savings can be **$1B.** Assaults in Victoria, are estimated at 257,000 per year. Arterial street amenity has long been the highest traffic priority for municipalities. Emissions and air quality are issues.

Attempts to improve existing transport systems are expensive but not effective. The 90km Suburban Rail Loop does not improve access to the CBD, is a disjointed system, will not even improve the suburban trip speed by cars nor trains, it is a relatively small part of trip lengths and it's cost is exhorbitant. It is not nimble and only delivers within 1,600m at NEIC's. SRL's opportunity costs are sufficient to fund very high speed rail to all Victorian towns of 500 population.

Aerial podcars are the only mode with reasonable prospects of providing good urban transport and of seriously reducing the subsidies, the road toll, assaults, degraded amenity and emissions. They are four times faster than cars, pleasant, private, with personal seamless routes, extremely reliable, of high capacity, and profitable, yet priced less than other options.

But aerial podcars are an immature mode and need to be brought into production with the highest quality. This just needs common sense, based on our experience with existing transport, and using a due diligence process.

Requirements of Aerial Podcars for better Service than Cars

Aerial podcars have **very low costs** because the vehicles are light weight and suspended, and their speed is constant. Their costs are an order lower than other transport modes, such that they can make a **substantial profit**. Businesses that make a profit expand and **create more jobs** than those needing subsidies. There is no call for government funding, but revenue is created.

Aerial podcars are the **size of a car**, are for private hire, and have personal routes for security and speed. Trips can traverse the shortest routes, **seamlessly, across a network**. Guideways are grade-separated with interchanges, like freeways. **Fully automatic** vehicles are super-safe, **four times faster than cars and reliable** at 70kph, **saving $22B** in delay costs. They deliver closer to destinations, land within malls and at the foyer of buildings.

Aerial podcars are a scenic and pleasant experience, yet not intrusive nor polluting, and attract **80% of traffic** from cars, and all patronage from public transport. They carry **freight**. They improve amenity of arterial streets, reduce the number of assaults and reduce the **road toll by 80%, saving $1B.**

Vendor - Industry Review & Offerings

All urban transport is **at very high risk of disruptive developments** in aerial podcars. Praetor Capital's report on personal rapid transit (PRT) notes the beginnings of a boom in podcar investments. Aerial podcars are available from many vendors, including but not limited to Metrino, Jpods, Vuba and TransitX.

Metrino has the most transparent performance and costings, where **operating costs are 5c per vehicle-km, capital costs are $13M per km** for two-way guide-way including 3 stops and 100 vehicles, vehicle speed is 70kph and flow rates are one vehicle per second. Track is **10m high, grades are 100% and stops are on the ground.**

Jpods has operating costs of 2c per pax-km, vehicle speed is 72kph but stops are serial. Track is 7m high, grades are flat and **stops are elevated.**

Vuba has low operating costs, 6 passengers/vehicle, **shared vehicles**, available within a minute, flow rates are 14,000 pax/hour. Track is 7m high, grades are flat and **stops require lifts**.

TransitX proposes a 3,486km network for Melbourne with 132,000 pods, within 10 minutes walk of 7,040 stops. Capital costs are $4M per km of dual track, $7,000/pod, vehicle speed is 72kph. Track is 7m high, grades are flat, **stops are serial and pods are lowered to the ground**.

Profit Potential

An 733km grid network for Melbourne podcars would have the current fare structure of 21c per km that covers operating cost of 5c per veh-km, capital repayment of 10c per veh-km, and 6c per veh-km profit. Further revenue sources from freight distribution, and from in-vehicle personalised advertising would be bonus factors, perhaps with **profits exceeding 15c per veh-km. Annual profit of $1B** is estimated for the 733km network.

Individual routes would be profitable, building towards a grid network that would be highly profitable, building further to a finer network with better service that would grow profits but not the profit rate.

Who gets the profits depends upon the business plan and 5% to the State as land owner, 15% to the vendor-operator, and 80% to reinvest in expansion towards a 1,745km network for better service is proposed. The State therefore gets $50M profit and avoids of public transport subsidies of $5B. The major benefit is not the profit, but the $22B saving in trip time to the travelling public, beside the $1B saving in road toll costs.

Risks of Obsolescence, of sub-par Quality.

Extending the current public transport systems, that will soon become obsolete, is **very high risk**, running up debts of $5B per year that should become stranded **without revenue**. The Suburban Rail Loop project cost is $35B for 26km for the first part of a 90km project. Trip times along the route average 60kph, there is no seamless connection to the rail network and proximity is only within 1,600m at the National Employment and Innovation Clusters. Even along the route, **podcars** would be faster, and would deliver **to the doorsteps**, making the SRL slower, obsolete and without custom.

Podcars would also eventually collect **from the entire city, seamlessly**, integrating and speeding up trips that are proposed to be disjointed by the SRL.

Even a crude attempt to introduce aerial podcars would be much more successful. A **733km grid** network skeleton, twice the size of the 388km urban rail network would only cost **$10B of deficit finance**, incurring **no cost** to government. The risk with this new technology is that the development of the system might be rushed and the quality not be as high as specified herein such that mode change might not be fully realised.

Patronage Estimate.

What proportion of people would choose podcars that are **scenic, four times faster, half the cost and more reliable than cars**? This is extrapolating far beyond the scope of mode choice models but is probably in the **realm of 80%**, subject to adequate **quality and marketing**. The quality should be assured with a 1km test track. Marketing should include exposure by installing an internal system within the airport. Trains, trams and buses average only 10kph, do not have the benefits of proximity, and lack privacy, so they should lose all patronage and revenue. Because the existing transport, including cars, is so poor, podcars would be so very disruptive.

Compare the performance of cars with aerial podcars for radial trips within 10km of the CBD, where it really matters. Cars average 15kph, but are also subject to frequent traffic incidents and road closures, their marginal operating costs are 30c per km, parking is time consuming and costs are $20 per day, but they have the advantage of parking at the place of residence. Aerial podcars would average 60kph, are extremely reliable, and have fares to match the current fare levels of 21c/passenger-km. Podcars have ruling speed of 70kph and 15kph for bikes or electric scooters at trip ends would make average trip speeds 60kph.

Freight patronage is not estimated but needs to be included.

Implementation Strategy - Seek, Develop, Market, with Prudence

Any government that is confident of their requirements can probably acquire a bespoke system of the highest quality at a much lower cost, by **taking on board the risk of development** as is proposed, but still without a requirement for funding, just a guarantee to **counter Sovereign risk**. The engineering of the concept is available and it is only a matter of reaching an acceptable business plan with a vendor.

Aerial podcars are an immature mode and competition between different concepts has not yet happened. The author has reasoned for a particular specification that is not yet available from any vendor. Those vendors and their investors have taken enormous risk with their investment and are deserving of high rewards, that translate to higher costs for transport, but the quality of service can be easily improved. Compare the requirements of the specification herein with the offerings.

Strategy Choices, Enterprise or Waste

The proposition that due process would yield an **aerial podcar no-funding option** with a vision for a complete service in the near future of a very high quality transport standard must surely be **economically attractive and with lesser risk.**

A number of choices exist. One is to continue to extend current systems at a cost of **$5B per year, that will surely become obsolete**, while waiting for a podcar market to develop, expecting the podcar competition to shake out the poor quality options. There are strong vested interests in cars and trains and this process may be lengthy and not well managed by governments, perhaps as badly as they are managing the current road systems and congestion.

Another option is to invoke a DARPA type competition to sort out the technology. The author has reasoned for a detailed specification that should suit Melbourne, with an emphasis on apparent direct service. Readers might review the specification and come up with a host of variations.

Promotion to Introduce and Reinforce

Marketing the new system is important, through both familiarity and appearance. **Familiarity** can be achieved by using the system to replace the existing internal bus service from the car park at the airport and providing a direct personal service from the current car park stations to each specific airline check-in, coming down through the roof, with return trips from the baggage carousels for arrivals.

The broader network should **appear to be direct and efficient** by having two-way track, having a primary direction for stops, having two-way access to stops, and having stabling at stops for assurance of availability, because it is necessary to mimic or exceed the convenience of a car.

Failure of the Market and Leadership

With such a superior trip speed and with prospects for highly profitable operation, there is **market failure** and it is assumed that the main cause of this is **Sovereign risk**. Sovereign risk clearly applies to projects dependent upon Government approval to their operation, approval for use of the right of way and it's cheap rental.

To overcome this, the Government should **guarantee the finance** for an initial 1km test track, for replacing the internal airport bus service, and for a 21km pilot route to the airport. The Government should also guarantee the availability of **public right of way** for the test track, the pilot route and for every future route at a **fixed rental of 5%** of net profits. The Government should support value capture for the provision of stops.

The Government should contract to direct 80% of net profits for reinvestment to **intensify the network**, building towards the 1,745km network, subject to each addition increasing the overall profit. The 15% balance of net profit goes to the Vendor-operator.

Due Diligence to Verify Each Step

The Government should call for expressions of interest to build **a test track, an internal airport service, and a pilot route to the airport** of an aerial podcar system with a guarantee to under-write the cost for the test track, the internal airport service and the pilot route. There would be an obligation to expand to a complete network for Melbourne, subject only to expected increase in profitability with each addition to the network. The minimum quality of the service should be as specified herein.

The business plan should be verified by independent Consultants as delivering **high quality service and highly profitable** before proceeding, and that plan should be confirmed after the test track. The business plan should include freight and in-vehicle advertising. The project should be deficit financed. The sharing of profits will depend upon business realities, taking into account that the government is under-writing the initial development risk.

Test Track for Quality and Approvals

A test track is essential to refine the **quality of service** that the system delivers, to confirm the **costs** and to obtain **approvals**. There are multiple known ways to provide the many functions required, such as steep descent grades, in-vehicle switching, control of merging with one second spacing, and silent track joins, but these must be demonstrated.

All variations to the design must be subject to vendor approval, because Consultants are not that independent of Government, and because there is a history of podcar impediment by weight increase with Taxi2000 and weight is critical. It is about enterprise.

The test track is an important hold point in the due diligence process.

Take Away

Podcars will save the community **$22B/year** in trip time and **$1B/year** in road crash costs. They will improve: access to jobs; safety; security; amenity; service; performance; and revenue. Profitable transport will **create more jobs**.

Podcars are certain to reduce risk by cancelling the expensive, obsolete Suburban Rail Loop that will under-perform, saving **$5B/year**.

Find a vendor with a high profitability business plan that meets the specification, has a reasonable allocation of profits, and back them with prudence and due diligence.

Alternative Networks - Deliver Affordable Transport where Needed for all Victoria

Business Case, based only on Fares

A 733km urban grid network with stops at 2km proximity would be highly profitable and a more intense 1,745km urban network with stops at 500m proximity may be profitable (the top half of the table). The 733km network is self-sufficient and would be connected to all commercial and significant centres.

This profitability relates only to the network operator and fare revenue. It does not account for $22B savings in congestion costs, $1B savings in road toll, $5B savings in government subsidies, avoidance of project funding, nor revenue from freight or in-vehicle advertising, nor the benefits of urban development. Based on these coarse and incomplete estimates, only the 733km urban network is highly profitable. It should be brought into production using due process and then expanded to a 1,745km network as profits permit.

Route	Length km	Daily Traffic	Stops No.	Podcars No.	Profit %
Melbourne@2km	733	40,000	2,200	73,000	46
Melbourne@0.5km	1,745	20,000	5,000	83,000	-21
Regional Stubs	300				
Regional@0.5p/m	797	6,000	800	22,000	-86
Regional, other	5,577	700	5,000	10,000	-98
Regional Total	6,674		3,000	95,000	

The Suburban Rail Loop business case notes the poor quality transport in Melbourne, then proceeds to not examine the transport options but to propose planning and develpment of National Employment and Innovation Clusters. Any business case using benefits from developments as justification is flawed if it does not first consider transport alternatives, including aerial podcars.

The transport aspects of the SRL business case are deeply flawed because it proposes obsolete technology that does not have seamless integration with the existing rail network. As a result trip speeds on the SRL average 60kph, but there are huge delays to links with the existing rail network, that has a much lower trip speed. Further, the proposal to deliver passengers within 1,600m at the NEIC's does not meet reasonable transport objectives and does not compare with delivery to each building foyer by podcars.

Scenic Rail Melbourne - 2km Grid

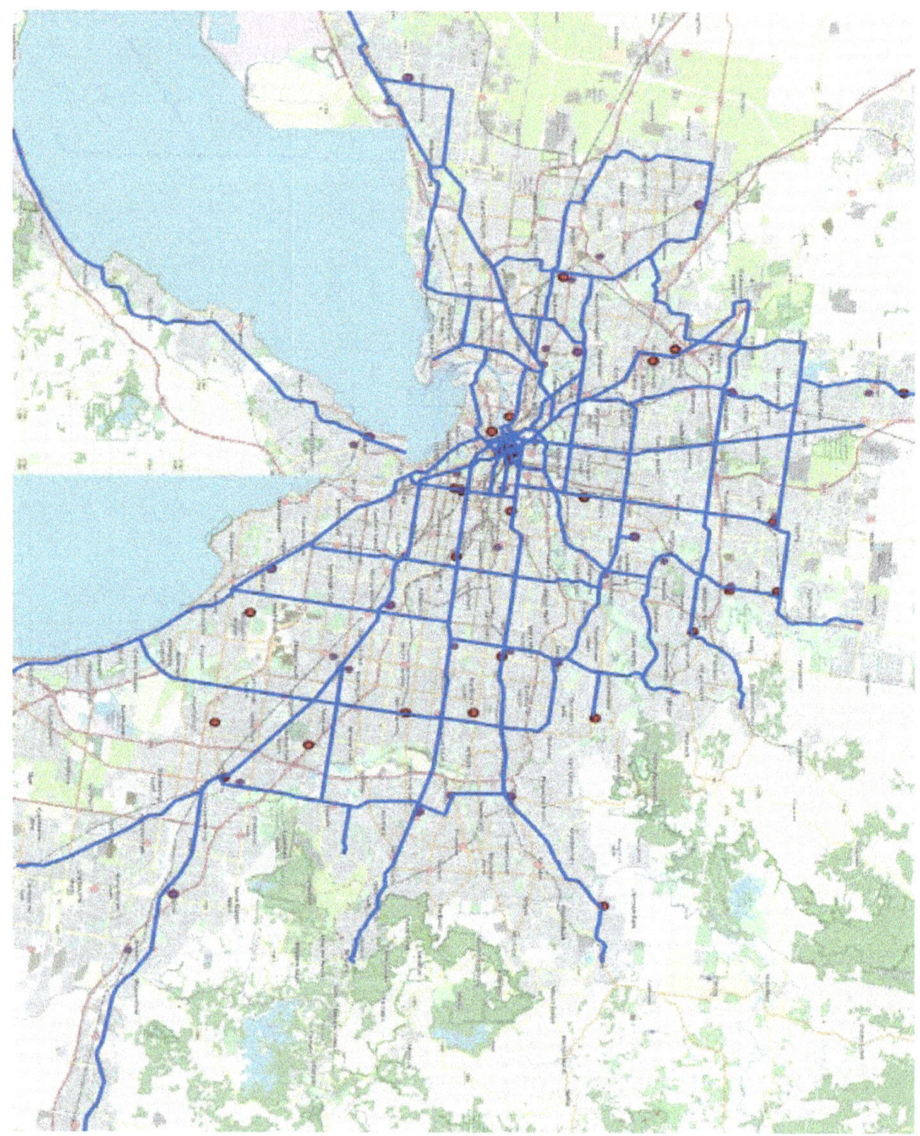

This map of Scenic Rail Melbourne shows a 733km **grid** network, **twice the length** of the existing 388km rail network, with stops typically within 2km, that would be **highly profitable, self-funded** and built in a few years.

Trips would be on personal routes, direct between any two stops, seamlessly navigating the shortest set of routes. The routes overlay arterial roads, not railways nor freeways, because that is where the destinations are. Local consultation will surely improve detail of access to all commercial and community centres. Podcars should come down through the roof to stop(s) within all malls.

This grid network forms the skeleton of the larger 1,745km network with 500m proximity. Drawn in QGIS with Open Street Map.

Closer Network for Melbourne - 500m Proximity

This map extends Scenic Rail Melbourne to a 1,745km network, four times the length of the existing rail network, with stops typically within 500m, funded with surplus profits from the basic network.

The 733km network is certain to be profitable and the network may extend to 1,745km with increasing profit. They are of different character, being grid and radial respectively. The basic grid provides ability to deliver quite efficient routes between any two stops and the larger network is the grid with the addition of many radial small off-shoots that have the main function of reducing the stop proximity from 2km to 500m.

It is prudent to start with the more profitable option, and have a plan to extend the network subject to each addition increasing profit. Drawn in QGIS with Open Street Map.

High Speed Urban & Rural Service

Serious consideration should be given to providing a **low cost, high speed service** for both longer urban trips and for rural Victoria. It is worthy of conducting a due process to **research** and develop a technology for the purpose, based on a high speed version of aerial podcars, or the equivalent, but founded on a strong business case. This investigation should start when the test track has been completed.

Closer Network for Melbourne - 500m Proximity

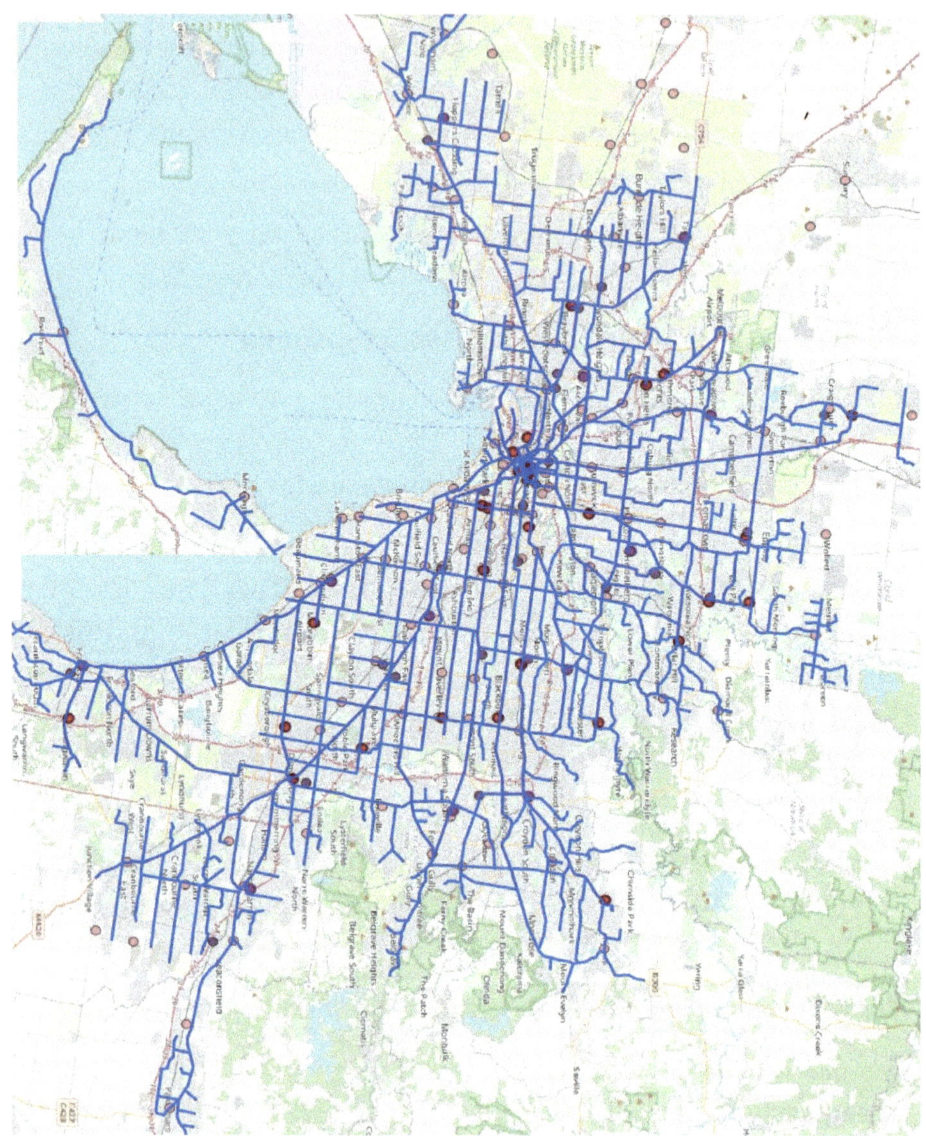

One option is to use platoons of podcars at higher speeds and another is to use drones or hyper-loops at much higher speeds. Up to **250kph on podcar guide-ways** seems achievable. It may involve podcars operating in trains, on special guideways, with special bogies, without the need to change vehicle, and at **premium prices to cover increased costs**.

Regional stubs would be duplicates of the urban network where the regional service was of a different character or speed, making it possible to traverse the city at high speed.

Transit X offers 242kph high speed service and Skytran 160kph, but these should be regarded as research rather than development, based on the **absence of real world examples**. It would be prudent to first develop the urban network, and then research a high speed arterial function for the urban network, possibly with a pilot route to Geelong, because that is the location of high demand. Then extend it to other rural areas. Aerial podcars have a cost advantage and a safety advantage over trains. Bullet trains can achieve 300kph.

Podcar routes to Geelong, Sunbury and Melton may be profitable. Podcar routes to Ballarat, Ocean Grove, Drysdale, Leopold, Torquay, Bendigo, Bacchus Marsh, Traralgon, and Whittlesea would require some funding. Podcar routes to Shepparton and Albury would require significant funding. Route length is the main cost as operating costs could be recovered at current fare rates. The rural network would cost $10M/km to build. Separate consideration of tourist investments would be warranted using a better knowledge of the tourist business plan. But that still only provides a radial network.

If alternatively, drones the size of a car became available with speeds of 200kph, no network costs or radial restrictions would apply, but operating costs would be much higher.

Victoria Rural

Rural service would require higher speeds and was **not developed as a proposal**. That may require a capital cost **subsidy of about $50B**. Then operation of the network at cost would provide cheap instant transport access, 24/7, to the entire rural area of Victoria, for schools, shops, health, employment, business, freight and tourism.

The total high speed length has been amended to 5,092km to include 305km of high speed in Melbourne. It assumes podcars at higher speeds. The rural network may have one standard vehicle and one standard speed or not. Towns 500+ are shown green, 1,000+ are shown blue, and 6,000+ are shown red. Drawn in QGIS with Open Street Map.

This is an extension of the 733km grid of Scenic Rail Melbourne with 797km of Scenic Rail Victoria that has a higher passenger loading, both drawn in blue, and a major extension by 3,990km, drawn in red, to service all towns with 1,000 population with a radial, not grid network. The radial network would provide access to major centers for equity. It would provide waiting vehicles, 24/7, for trips between any two stops in the whole network. Vehicles would accommodate bikes, electric scooters or wheelchairs for the "last mile " of trips.

Further developmental investment would be required to give accessibility for remote areas and for tourism. The proposition is that subsidy of the rural network would provide tourist access to rural areas and freight delivery to Melbourne of produce. For schools, a podcar network, the size of the Highway system, as mapped, was considered, with feeder routes in the form of off-road cycle paths for safety.

Specification - Quality Transport Service.

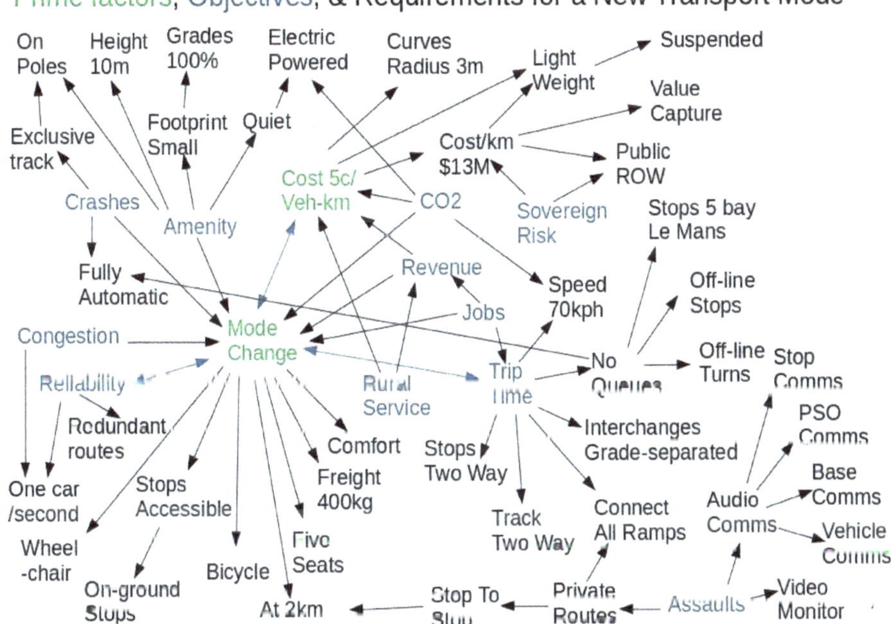

Mindmap of Requirements for Aerial Podcars.

Podcar vendors offer a variety of options, that taken as a whole, would provide the highest quality of service. Requiring the best service with a bespoke system would have very little impact on costs but would attract more custom. This mindmap of requirements is derived from worthy transport objectives. All the items are considered essential, but not yet available from any one vendor.

Marketing of the New Technology

The specification is based on marketing aerial podcars as a much more efficient and more pleasant mode than cars, so every opportunity is taken to present them as **direct and flexible**, with direct connections, to avoid the equivalent of one-way streets, and to have two-way access to stops, so that the nearest stop is relevant.

They must be very accessible, are free of rider restrictions, are quite scenic, and able to venture where cars cannot go, specifically to be **very nimble** and come down through the roof and land within a shopping mall, or to deliver to the forecourt of each major building.

Setting the objective speed at 60kph average, for public transport, four times faster than cars, necessitates direct routes, avoidance of serial queues, absence of capacity restrictions and a comprehensive network, with stop proximity in the suburbs at least within 2km but preferably within 500m. This means two-way travel; direct access to stops; grade separation between routes; direct connections at interchanges; stops off-line and turns off-line. Limit speed to 70kph to maintain capacity and keep costs low.

Directional capacities must be 3,600 vehicles per hour to achieve the transport task. Capacity twice that proposed has been proven with Taxi2000, but is not preferred, because having multiple routes down parallel streets delivers more proximate service and has redundancy when routes are off-line for maintenance. Podcars have slightly lower capacities than trains and freeways, but are better able to deliver traffic down more routes, and closer to destinations, since they are 20 times cheaper, and satisfy amenity. "Last mile" travel for the 2km or 500m trip ends by bikes or electric scooters is necessary for highly efficient trips. The intent is to service all commercial centres.

Vehicles, of Car Size & Adaptable

Podcars must have capacity for wheelchairs and mobility scooters for accessibility, carry bikes for trip speed, seat five people for convenience, carry 400kg freight containers for revenue and amenity, have heating and cooling and be as quiet as a Prius for amenity. Freight distribution is highly desirable, so carrying mobility scooters is just a matter of design. One standard vehicle size would improve availability, scheduling and trip speed, enabling ranks at stops for immediate service.

Podcars must have video monitoring for personal security, have 220nm uv lighting for sanitising, be fully automatic and on exclusive track for safety, have private hire for security, have private routes for trip speed, be electric powered and have low particulate emissions for amenity, and be suspended for light weight and low cost. 220nm uv lighting kills all germs and viruses but does not cause harm to people.

Track, Unobtrusive, Nimble & Off-line Turns

Podcar guide-way is to be two-way, on poles to avoid obstruction to road traffic, located 10m high to avoid visual blight and to permit trees below, have steep 100% grades to permit stops on the ground with a small footprint and without intrusion or severance. Track joins must be quiet.

Podcar guide-way must have off-line stops and off line turns to avoid queues and to maintain trip speed and capacity, to have flow rates of one vehicle per second each way for adequate capacity, to permit tight 3m radius curves to fit turning guide-ways into narrow reserves.

Podcar guide-way must have grade-separated interchanges to maintain trip speed and capacity, to be in public right-of-way for low cost, and to have redundant routes for reliability.

One-way track would be indirect like one-way streets. Flat track would require expensive lifts at stops or stops would take up too much space.

Stops, Low Target, Two-Way, Stabling

Stops are to be on-ground for accessibility, to have a low visual target for amenity, to not obstruct arterial traffic, to have vehicles waiting for security and speed, and to have five Le-mans style bays for trip speed, with stops spaced at 300m in the suburbs and at 100m in commercial areas for security and speed.

Stops must serve one main direction so that vehicles entering the stop return to whence they came, for trip speed, and have U-turn ability to cover both directions. On average, 30 podcars should be stabled at every stop where they will be needed. This is probably best done at height with another U-turn.

Detailed Objectives for all Transport Problems & Solutions

Fast Trips, 60kph Average

Podcars would average **60kph, four times faster than cars,** where and when it matters. The charts show current trips less than 10km, trips 10-20km, and trips beyond 20km for cars and for public transport. Trips for **cars averaged 15kph, 23kph and 38kph,** for the inner, middle and outer trips respectively. Similarly, trips for **public transport averaged 10kph, 18kph and 23kph.**

Infrastructure Australia in their 2015 audit, estimated delay cost for trips in Melbourne to be $3B in 2011, growing to **$9B in 2031**. Delay cost was estimated by comparing peak period trip times with off-peak period trip times. This method is fully slanted toward the current transport system and grossly under-estimates the actual trip cost. If however, the trip times were compared to those available from aerial podcar transport, that average 60kph, the delay cost would have been **$22B in 2031**, just for peak periods.

The first three charts show existing trip time by cars & podcars. Trip times are charted for the PM peak in blue, for the AM peak in red, for the off-peak in yellow and are compared to the 60kph podcar times in green.

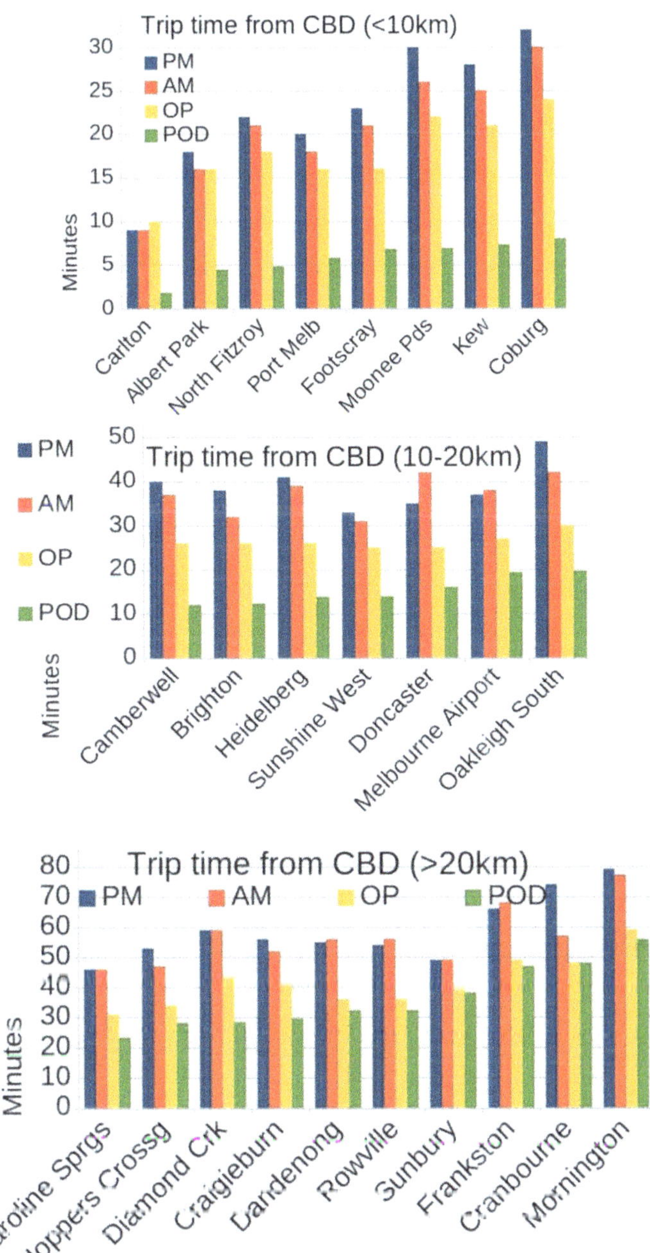

The Grattan Institute report in 2017 studied trip times for radial routes to the Melbourne CBD and the same set of radial routes are used here. There are delays due to traffic incidents and road works, and circumferential trips, that are not measured.

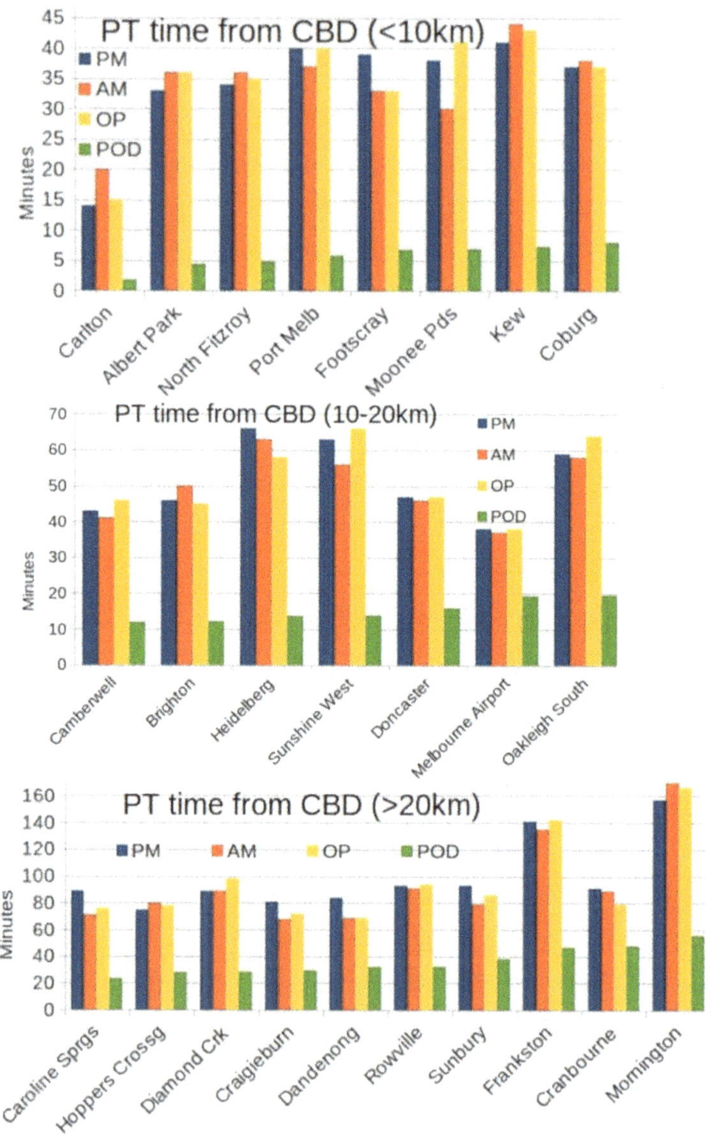

Public transport trip times are from the PTV journey planner. Melbourne public transport services are slow, suffer from cancellations, are designed for passengers to stand, are over-crowded, create huge pedestrian flows and require change of vehicle.

Cars are an inalienable right of freedom that should not be taken away from people, even if they are slow and have issues of reliability, cost, safety, emissions and intrusion. But traffic would be attracted out of cars by podcars with **superior service, based on cost, trip time, and reliability**. Using a World Bank survey of price elasticities of demand, it is estimated that 80% of traffic would be attracted to aerial podcars but a few functions would remain best serviced by cars or trucks.

Reliability, Automatic, Redundancy, Exclusive Track, Sensors

Proven methods to achieve reliability include: vehicles being **fully automatic;** routes having **redundancy** and excess capacity; and all control and propulsion components being reliable and having redundancy. For reliability, there must be multiple sensors, control systems, **exclusive track,** and **no serial queues,** but parallel off-line stops, off-line turns, and grade separated interchanges.

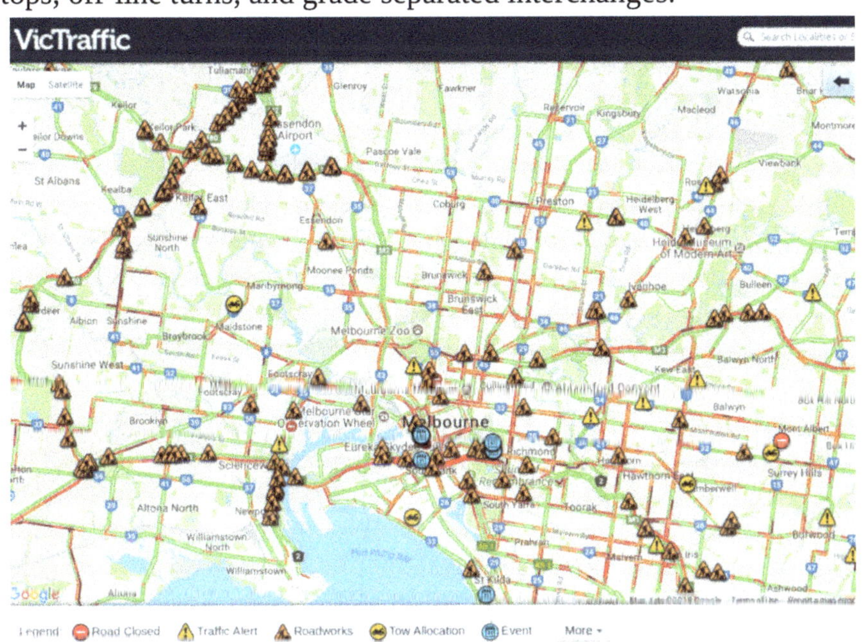

Roadworks, are widespread and traffic incidents abound. Reliability for road trips is not measured, but poor, given that one can rely on a number of traffic incidents in every peak period, but not on a predictable trip time. Reliability has not been established for Melbourne because congestion and road safety are much more immediate problems, that are yet to be resolved before reliability.

Cheap - Low Cost Trips, Light Weight Vehicles, Smooth Running

Flying over the top of all obstacles, like "the Jetsons", but hung from a guide-way, in a cost-efficient vehicle, not high energy flying, has been proven to be feasible at an average speed of 60kph. **Suspended vehicles** like Metrino only **weigh 300kg**, and have half the weight of on-ground systems like the 850kg Ultra, requiring lighter structures and so have half the cost, enabling costs so low as to be **highly profitable with current fare levels** for an 733km network with stops at 2km proximity.

Costs are ten times cheaper than cars. Low cost vehicles on exclusive track, operated at **express and constant speed** between trip ends, can cost only 5c/vehicle-km, and two-way track, 10m high, mounted on poles can cost only $13M/km, including 3 stops and 100 vehicles, using costs derived from Metrino. Current fare revenue of 21c/km covers operating cost of 5c/veh-km, capital repayment of 10c/veh-km, and 6c/veh-km profit. There are **further revenue sources** that must be achieved from freight and advertising. Metrino vehicle capacities are quoted and one standard size. Jpods and Vuba are similar. TransitX has a variety of vehicles. Note that current fares per person are being compared with costs per vehicle.

The Australian Infrastructure Plan, Figure 5.4 shows that **cost recovery** for public transport is only **22%**, and recommends value capture, higher fares, and improved efficiency. Fares do not even cover operating costs. But higher fares are not appropriate, better to cut costs.

Crashes - Automatic Vehicles, Exclusive Track

Any involvement of humans in road safety will always be a concern, and only fully automatic systems on exclusive track have proven to satisfy the most stringent safety standards, as exampled by Morgantown West Virginia group rapid transit and Ultra rapid transit at Heathrow. Attracting 80% of traffic away from cars, on to safe transport, would save 2,000 casualty crashes per year, valued at **$1B/year**.

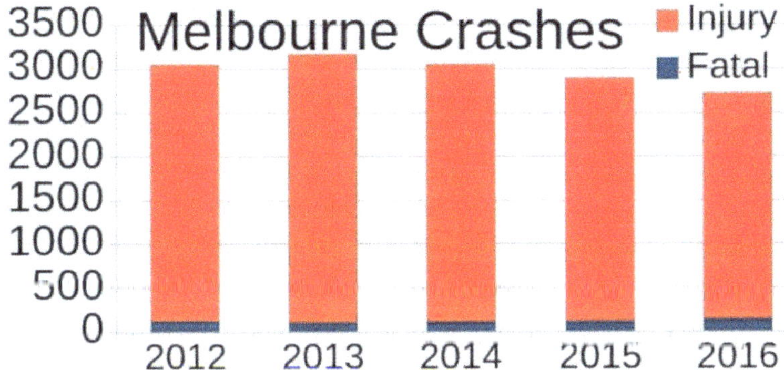

There are **3,000 hospitalised** road casualties per year resulting from 2504 crashes in Melbourne in 2017. This included 104 fatalities, 269 cyclists and 397 pedestrians.

People have the freedom to drive relatively dangerous cars, and motorbikes, with no automatic speed control, nor red light control, as is now proven possible with driver-less cars, to drive drunk, or under the influence of drugs, unlicensed or unregistered, with limited eyesight or medical conditions, to engage in high speed chases with police, and the existential rules are to give them a slap on the wrist, even for repeat offenders. Regulation of car drivers is a community decision and is moderated by the paucity of other options available. But the 3,000 casualties is a significant risk that should **never be acceptable**.

There are practical limits to the safety of driver-less cars. For perfect safety, driver-less cars can only travel at 10kph near pedestrians and 1m clear of cyclists. This is not acceptable to car companies. Driver-less cars can not be complemented by driver-less cyclists and driver-less pedestrians. Driver-less cars require a driver for the foreseeable future. The safety benefits of driver-less cars are worthwhile, yet not sufficient.

Assaults, Private Vehicles, No Waiting, Video Monitoring

Only private vehicles will suffice. They should have **personal routes** from origin to destination, **without vehicle change**; and to **avoid waiting** should always be available at stops, that are at **close proximity** to origins and destinations. Proximity within 100m at destinations and 300m near homes, would minimise exposure. Speed between the stop and trip end using a bike or scooter should also reduce exposure, and vehicles should accommodate mobility scooters.

Current projects for public transport increase exposure to strangers, with high volume transport, designed for crush loading, requiring more changes of vehicle, having greater wait times, having longer distances to walk, and very little video surveillance. This standard of security will **never be desirable** for the public and reliance on PSO's without structural changes to the system is not enough.

Video monitoring with audio communication is available for inside and outside of aerial podcars and at stops. Communication with the control room and with PSO's should be provided. Real-time facial recognition and integration with public lighting should also be provided. Privacy concerns associated with facial recognition and video recording will need to be taken on board with appropriate use and storage of the information, under the supervision of Police. Vehicles should transport offenders to custody. To counter domestic violence, word recognition software should identify lack of respect and "call it out", progressing to reporting and follow-up.

From the ABS survey, assaults in Victoria, were estimated at **257,000 per year**, and for females: 38% felt unsafe while walking, but 33% felt safe; 11% felt unsafe waiting at stops, but 22% felt safe; and 27% felt unsafe on public transport, but 24% felt safe. Of the violence toward females, 91,000 was from known persons and 32,000 from strangers.

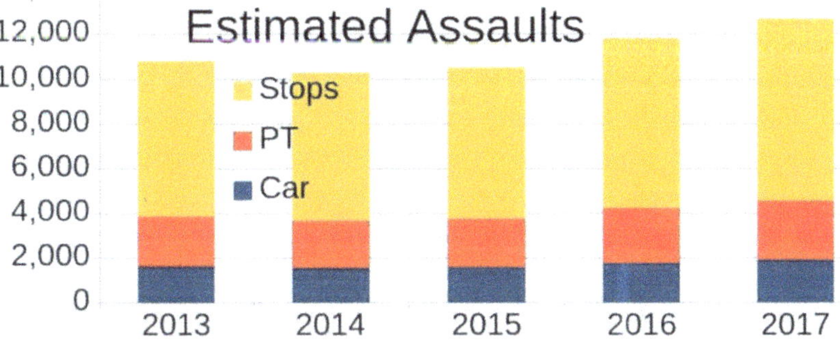

There is considerable under-reporting of assaults. Charges for assaults are recorded by police, and were previously dissected by cars, public transport and the street. Walking to transport or waiting at stops were not separately identified. Estimates shown here, are related to transport, are made from assaults by type, and are increasing. Recent reporting of the charges is dissected into domestic violence and stranger violence categories, with half the assaults being in each. Protective Service Officers have been used to patrol train stations, but they can't be everywhere. Low proportions of people feel safe on public transport at night. Costing of assaults has not included all factors and the cost of assaults in Melbourne is estimated at $60M, much less than crash or delay costs.

Amenity, Fewer Cars, Unobtrusive Structures, Quiet Transport

It is imperative that the volume of **car traffic be reduced** on amenity grounds. The sheer quantity of traffic makes it impractical to set aside adequate space and safety for pedestrians and cyclists. The traffic noise, fumes and intimidation mitigates against full use of the street for commercial and social activities.

Oppressive structures are not acceptable but **slender unobtrusive** alternatives such as this podcar **guide-way, located 10m high**, would be, if **100% grades to stops** at ground level are used to provide accessibility and avoid severance of one side of the street from the other. Podcars must be as **quiet as a Prius** and are light weight, and electric with steel wheels so have minimal particulate emission.

Arterial street amenity has long been the highest traffic priority for municipalities, and was second only to funding in a report based on a survey of 60 Mayors and 60 City Engineers. It has been neglected, is poor and deteriorating, Visual blight has forced demolition of raised grade separations. The figure shows a controversial rail project, popular with the travelling public, but local residents needed to be bought out.

Stops should present a minimal visual intrusion, video surveillance is provided at stops, and people do not need to shelter at stops, so stops should have no top nor sides. Stops should be integrated with the destination, be it a mall or foyer and they should avoid exposure to or impact on arterial traffic by location within a side street, not on an arterial road. Podcar images are from Metrino.

A nominal **5 bays** have been assumed on the ground at each stop. Contrary to the example shown, each stop should have a **primary direction**, where the departure returns from whence it came. Further, a **U-turn** should be provided at height so that the secondary direction can also access the stop, and finally, a further U-turn should be provided at height to accommodate **stabling** for 30 vehicles at each stop.

Noise levels on arterial streets often exceed criteria set for freeways, but there are no remedial options offered and set-backs are not practical. Air pollution, including fumes and particulates, is often at levels that impact health, again with no practical response. There are some ingrained, expedient, but unsafe practices, such as high speed, and mixing of cars with pedestrians and cyclists. Planning is anti-social and allocates the highest density living to the most degraded streets, so excessive car traffic and speed means that children can no longer play in the street. Space requirements for car parking is substantial. Errant vehicles are a constant threat to life and property. Reduction of car traffic is essential.

Congestion Removal

Attracting 80% of traffic to aerial podcars would have a major impact on congestion and trip time, **saving $22B per year.**.

Infrastructure Australia's Audit Volume 2, Figure 62 is shown. Delay estimates are grossly under-estimated as previously discussed. Poor planning has resulted in inadequate transport reserves, that would be too disruptive to widen. The only conventional options to remove congestion, above those described in Crafting Green Waves, are: to tunnel, involving excessive costs, and providing limited functionality; or to price travel, that reduces equity, and living standards. Congestion includes public transport over-loading.

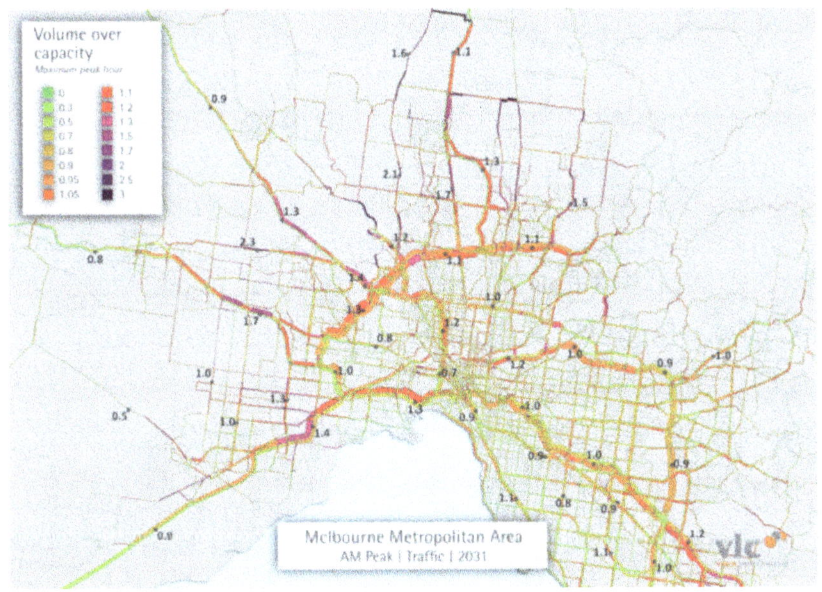

Emissions & Energy Reduction

CO_2 is an agreed problem and transport makes significant emissions. Any generation of energy involves creating emissions and reduced requirements for energy correspondingly reduces emissions, besides reducing costs. Podcars use **10 times less** energy than **cars** and **8 times less** than **trains.** Data source: Richard F. Di Bona, Ollie Mikosza.

Relative Energy Efficiency		
Mode	kwH per Pax-km	Ratio
Rail	0.512	8.4
Buses	0.773	12.7
Cars	0.644	10.6
Ultra	0.153	2.5
Metrino	0.061	1

Revenue, Profits & Effectiveness

Annual profit of $1B is estimated for the 733km network. Who gets the profits depends upon the business plan and 5% to the land owner, 15% to the vendor-operator, and 80% to reinvest in network expansion for better service is proposed. While the 733km network will be highly profitable, it only provides stops at 2km proximity. Profits should be used to extend the service, hopefully to the 1,745km network with stops at 500m proximity, subject to each addition adding to the total profits.

It is reasonable to regulate surplus profits towards that objective, but the mode should pay a nominal rental of 5% of profits for locating poles in public reserves. That would only provide revenue of $50M.

The main benefits accrue to the public in the form of $22B trip time saving and $1B safety. Another major benefit to the government is avoidance of $5B major expenditure on public transport, both in capital expenditure and operating subsidies. This should release funds for rural transport.

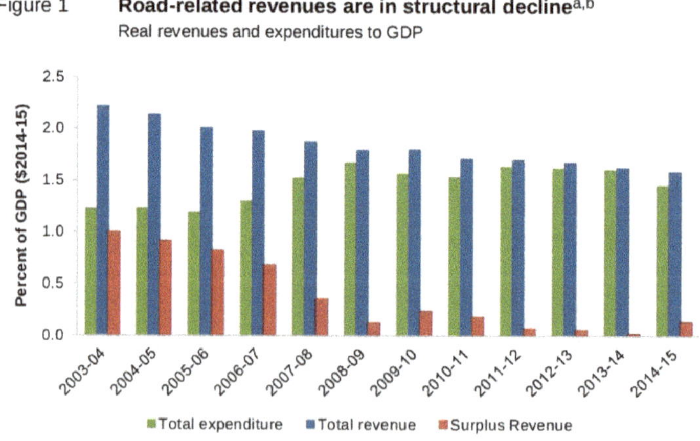

Figure 1   **Road-related revenues are in structural decline[a,b]**
Real revenues and expenditures to GDP

Road related revenues are in structural decline according to the Productivity Commission Review, Figure 1. The Commission recommends road pricing, that is regressive and gives lower service.

Job Creation, Profits & Effectiveness

The job creation potential of highly profitable aerial podcars has been evaluated, including from reinvestment, manufacturing and as a benefit for jobs saved by removing congestion and speeding up slow trips, as shown in the graph.

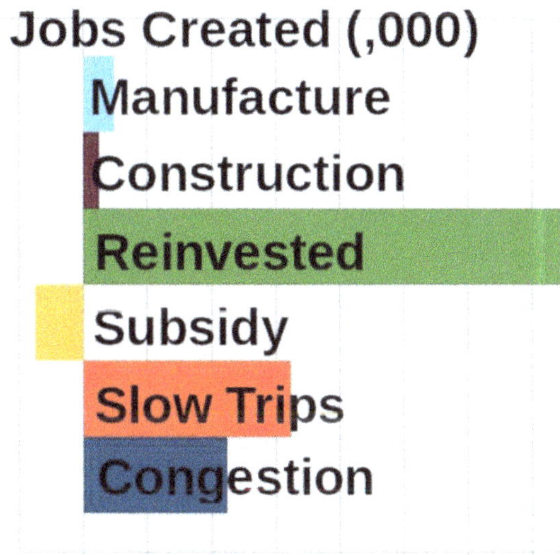

Good policy should **acquire training and investment**, as well as competition. There is an opportunity to invest in higher technology for transport. Jobs are created by manufacturing, construction and operation of transport, and by reinvesting transport profits.

Governments provide jobs for their mates, so jobs quoted are generally construction jobs. Jobs lost through congestion, slow trips, and even the increased congestion by the construction works are rarely quoted. Justification of business cases occurs after a decision to proceed, and in the light of fares covering only 22% of public transport costs, no PT project has credible direct profits. Fares do not even cover operating costs, and will never cover the larger construction costs.

Because PT requires massive subsidies, it represents jobs foregone. Just like any other business, if it makes a profit, more staff can be employed, and the greatest source for job creation would be the enormous profits expected from aerial podcars.

Jobs in manufacturing, particularly in the car industry, have been lost overseas, due to policy failure. It is essential to have efficiency in industry, such that can be obtained by enough competition, but that is invalid if it is based on slave labour rates, or on failure to equip or train staff, or on subsidies. The much lauded construction jobs are a very small portion of the real jobs picture, and they are probably dwarfed by the jobs wasted by the congestion that they cause.

Rural Service, Needs Enterprise & Equity

While some of the rural network can be profitable and self-funding, the speeds of the urban podcars are too slow for rural operations and no suitable solution for rural service was found, but further research is warranted.

Public transport is currently scheduled for sparse service particularly in the country, where commuting to Melbourne has the best service at ½ to 2 hour frequency, other services to Melbourne are daily, circulation within major towns is hourly and service between towns is weekly.

Although not an issue for Melbourne, the frequency and connectivity of public transport in rural areas of Victoria could not be described as a reasonable service. Whereas trains and buses can only recover 22% of costs in Melbourne, in rural areas with longer distances and lower patronage, the outcome is lower frequencies, if there is a service at all.

In locations where there is only one bus trip per week, it is not even practical to go shopping. Low cost transport should be considered a basic right, for equity. Aerial podcar operating costs are half the costs for a small car, so less than a car or taxi or bus.

Much of the rural network construction needs to be subsidised to provide equity for rural people, but once this is done, then the immediate availability of transport, 24/7, at half the existing running cost of a small car would be an enormous benefit for that rural populous, assuming a similar service to aerial podcars was adopted. The basis for subsidising rural service should include access to rural areas for tourism from the city and delivery of rural produce to the city.

Evaluation of Alternative Modes - Only One Solution

	Monorail	Car Share	Driverless	Pub.Trans.	Rd.Pricing	Cars	Ground Pod	Aerial Pod	Drones
Crashes	✗	✗✗	✓✓	✗	✗	✗	✗	✓✓	✗✗✗
Assaults	✗✗	✗✗	✗	✗✗	✗✗	✗	✗✗	✓✓	✗
Amenity	⊘	✗	✗	✗	✗	✗	⊘	✓✓	✗
Congestion	✗✗✗	✗✗	✗	✗✗	✓	✓	✗✗✗	✓✓✓	✓
Trip Time	✗✗✗	✗✗	✗	✗✗	✗	✓	✗✗	✓✓✓	✓
Revenue	✗✗✗	✗	✗	✗✗✗	✓	✗✗	✗✗	✓✓✓	✗
Jobs	✗✗	✗	✗	✗✗	✗	✗✗	✗✗	✓✓✓	✗
Reliability	✗✗	✗✗	✗	✗	✗	✓	✗	✓✓✓	✗✗
CO2	✗	✗	✗	✗	✗	✗	✗	✓✓✓	✗✗✗
Rural	✗✗✗	✓	✗	✗✗	⊘	✗	✗✗✗	✓✓✓	⊘

Comparison of Modes against Objectives

Monorail, car share, driver-less cars, trams-trains-buses, road pricing, better roads, Ultra podcars, aerial podcars, and drones are evaluated as options for transport. For each mode, a representative implementation was considered and its impact on the objectives for the full transport system assessed.

Aerial podcars best meet the objectives and could be **four times faster than cars**, extremely reliable, of high capacity, and profitable, yet priced less than other options. Aerial podcars are not as intrusive as other modes and could directly enter all commercial and social centres, without conflicting with other modes nor degrading the amenity.

Alternatives that provided major structures in an arterial network (monorail, Ultra) are not acceptable for amenity because of visual blight and because of reduction of road capacity. Alternatives that do not attract sufficient mode change away from cars (monorail, car share, driver-less cars, trams-trains-buses, road pricing, better roads, Ultra podcars, and drones) are not acceptable for amenity, despite the expedient current practice. Both these items should be fatal flaws.

Alternatives that do not make a profit (trams-trains-buses) are not financially viable, such that standards that apply for businesses should also rule them out, despite our current approach for public transport. Alternatives that lower the level of transport service (monorail, car share, driver-less cars, trams-trains-buses, road pricing, better roads, Ultra podcars, and drones) are not acceptable. **All alternatives except suspended podcars are therefore ruled out**. A realistic analysis of freight has not been included but aerial podcars can make some contribution and the conclusion is unlikely to be changed by its addition.

Monorail, Rejected

Elevated two-way monorail tracks would have substantial and expensive structures, but with narrower track than trains, suitable only for a network of principal routes, 800km in length, twice the length of the Metropolitan rail system, at a 2km proximity, with grade separation of cross routes, 1,000 elevated stops with lifts, and the "last mile" serviced by 1,300km of feeder modes such as bikes.

Flat vertical alignment dictates elevated stops. Vehicles will have high capacity, precluding personal routes, and requiring change of vehicle, in addition to changes for feeder modes. They will have serial and frequent stops, limiting capacity and trip speed. The structures will reduce the capacity of arterial roads. Monorail will not be able to attract many people away from cars because of cost, reliability, including of route interchange connections, and trip time. It is similar to elevated light rail.

It fails all objectives, has fatal flaws of visual blight, reduced road capacity, and not enough mode change. It gives worse service.

Car Share, Rejected

Car sharing reduces the cost of car trips, so increases the number of trips by car, and increases congestion and trip time.

It is a cheaper version of the taxi and also a version of "mobility as a service". Single hire is assumed with a driver required, direct routes and only one stop per trip.

It fails all objectives, and has a fatal flaw of not enough mode change. It gives worse service.

Driver-less Cars, Rejected

Driver-less cars are already safer than the normal car, and are likely to be introduced progressively over the next 30 years. For this assessment, driver assisted cars are assumed, but not for the poorest 40% of people. Functions assumed include lane keeping, and crash avoidance for rear-ends and with pedestrians.

The technology can permit close spacing at high speed on freeways, but not during lane changing, yet when mixed with pedestrians and cyclists, slow speeds are required for safety, to such an extent that capacity is reduced at critical arterial locations, congestion is increased, and mode shift is to public transport.

Car makers with deep pockets have an imperative to sell cars, and will continue to improve them to gain an edge over their competitors. Safety improvements will protect the occupants, but not necessarily cyclists and pedestrians. Shortcomings are hidden from public view, including impacts on capacity and safety where there are pedestrians and cyclists. Models of high capacity would rely on "driver-less" cyclists and "driver-less" pedestrians, an unlikely prospect. On freeways where existing lane-changing gaps are 0.3 seconds, driver-less cars can barely match that, but note that lane changing gaps of 0.3 seconds are the main cause of freeway crashes. Regulation of 1m spacing from cyclists would have serious implications for driver-less cars.

It fails nearly all objectives, but does something for safety, and has a fatal flaw of not enough mode change. It fails on equity.

Public Transport, Rejected

Public transport is a low quality service, not capable of attracting people away from cars, because it fails on cost, reliability and trip time. It does not provide a seat, requires vehicle change from high volume routes to and from low volume feeder routes, does not deliver door to door, creates excessive pedestrian flows and requires increasing subsidies. Proposed improvements in public transport involve higher capacities and less personal service.

There is no consideration of upgrading train technology to fully automatic control, nor to include extensive video monitoring. Trips involving more than one route are not seamless. There is no plan for spare capacity in peak periods, and planning is based on "crush" loading, so there will always be times when passengers can not all board, and are left at the stop.

It fails all objectives and has a fatal flaw of not enough mode change. It is not financially viable and delivers worse service.

Road Pricing, Rejected

Central city pricing is assumed. Road pricing forces people off cars and onto other, inferior modes, but improves the operating conditions for road-based transport in the central city, and requires greater investment in public transport.

Most successful road pricing is on an area basis, and that may still permit congestion, or it may be over-kill. Queue-jumping as described in Crafting Green Waves, is better tailored to where there are delays. Crafting green waves applies to all major traffic arteries, particularly freeway ramp metering, includes the whole Melbourne area, and can replace any proposed area pricing. Except where pricing is carefully targeted at congestion, pricing reduces the level of service. But this still only addresses congestion and would not do enough for trip time.

It fails all objectives, does something for congestion, and has a fatal flaw of not enough mode change. It delivers worse service.

Better Roads, Rejected

Crafting Green Waves should be applied to existing roads. Wider roads must now be made using property acquisition and that has insurmountable political negatives. Building additional roads in the developed city is quite expensive, often requiring tunnels.

Melbourne has a history of land development as described in The Land Boomers, and Power Without Glory, where developers have priority over planning. Road reservations have either not been made before development, or have been surrendered to development. New roads would be few in number and would provide a limited improvement to trips. Tunnels, combined with upgrading arterial roads within their existing footprint to 2-phase intersections, and metering, for both freeways and arterial roads, would increase capacity, and reduce congestion and trip time, but increase the number of trips by car.

It fails all objectives, does something for travel speed and reliability, but at huge cost, and has a fatal flaw of not enough mode change. It delivers worse service.

Ultra Supported Podcars, Rejected

Elevated two-way podcar tracks would have substantial and expensive structures, suitable only for a network of principal routes, 800km in length, twice the length of the Metropolitan rail system, at a 2km proximity, with at-grade intersections of cross routes, 1,000 elevated stops with lifts, and the "last mile" serviced by 1,300km of feeder modes such as bikes.

Flat grades dictate elevated stops. Vehicles will have small capacity, like cars, and similar track to cars, permitting personal routes within the podcar network, but with change of mode to feeder routes. They will have off-line stops but not off-line turns because of right of way width restrictions, limiting capacity and trip speed. The structures will reduce capacity of arterial roads. Supported podcars will be able to attract some people away from cars because of reliability and trip time, but because of vehicle weight and structure cost, their profitability is marginal.

It fails all objectives, including badly on amenity and has fatal flaws of visual blight, reduced road capacity, and not enough mode change. It gives worse service.

Aerial Podcars, the Only Acceptable Option

Elevated two-way podcar tracks would have slender and inexpensive structures, suitable for a network 800km in length, providing 2,400 stops on the ground at 2km proximity, better than metropolitan rail. The "last mile" is serviced by 1,300km of feeder modes such as bikes. But regulation of surplus profits to intensify the network to stops at 500m proximity is proposed.

Suspended vehicles permit steep vertical alignment and stops at ground level, with minimal footprint. Vehicles will have small capacity, like cars, and be highly manoeuvrable, permitting interchanges within narrow rights of way, and allowing personal routes, from origin to destination without stopping. They will have off-line stops, and off-line turns, giving high capacity and trip speed. The structures can be contained within the verge, side streets or shop fronts and must not reduce the capacity of arterial roads. Suspended podcars will be able to deliver from point to point with personal trips, like a car, and attract most people away from cars because of superior reliability, trip time, and cost, and because of low vehicle weight, 300kg, and smooth operation, their profitability is huge. They will have video monitoring.

It meets all 9 urban objectives, notably on amenity, and is by far the best of the alternatives.

Drones, Rejected

Electric passenger carrying drones are under development and are not yet available for deployment. There are major hurdles to overcome, relating to safety, air traffic control, capacity for transit, capacity for landing, and performance in the wind. 500 landing sites are assumed for Melbourne, associated with football grounds; requiring 2,000km of feeder services.

They are not much different to helicopters in regard to energy usage. Costs are likely to be 25c/veh-km capital cost and $1/veh-km operating cost. Drones will be able to attract 20% of traffic away from cars, due to the high speeds: 100kph, but are limited by the high cost, increased risk, and reliability as impacted by wind.

Example 1: Lilium, winged, $5M per plane, 300kph, $1/pax-km. Example 2: Ehang 184, $200k per drone, 100kph, 35c/pax-km, 40km range.

Drones are not available but if their hurdles can be overcome, they will fail all objectives but provide a high speed service to a select few. It has fatal flaws of not enough mode change and excessive energy use. It fails on equity.

Table of Contents

References

1. Google john cleeland youtube, click videos for simulations.

2. Metropolitan road traffic issues : a municipal view, 1988.

www.ingramcontent.com/pod-product-compliance
Lightning Source LLC
Chambersburg PA
CBHW050013040726
47599CB00014B/1366